TWO
ROMANTIC
TRIOS

THE STORY OF SIX PASSIONATE PEOPLE
WHO CHANGED THE WORLD OF MUSIC

SHERYL MACY

Published by
Allegro Publishing
Portland, Oregon

First Edition

Published by Allegro Publishing
Portland, Oregon

Manufactured in the United States of America

Library of Congress Catalog Card Number: 90-83621
Macy, Sheryl, 1950 -

Two Romantic Trios: The story of six passionate people who changed the
world of music.

ISBN   0-9627040-0-8   Paperback

CONTENTS

PRELUDE 1

THE FIRST TRIO 9

I MUSIC'S CHILDREN 11

II A ROMANTIC COMING OF AGE 23

III THE STRUGGLE FOR FULFILLMENT 51

IV JOY AND MADNESS 67

V TWO OLD FRIENDS 91

THE SECOND TRIO 107

VI BEAUTIFUL BABY 109

VII THE MAKING OF A MAESTRO 129

VIII A PASSION FOR OPERA 153

POSTLUDE 169

A A CONTEMPORARY CHRONOLOGY 173

B LISTENING TO THE ROMANTICS 187

C A MUSICAL VOCABULARY 195

D A READER'S BIBLIOGRAPHY 203

Two powerful men came to Vienna in May of 1809. Napoleon Bonaparte watched triumphantly as his artillery barrage destroyed the great city's defenses. Ludwig van Beethoven huddled in his cellar with pillows clutched over his painfully inflamed ears to protect them from the noise of Napoleon's bombardment. Different as they might seem, both men would have a dramatic effect on the music of their age.

Napoleon's influence was unintentional. The political upheavals he set in motion created a new society in which artists could create.

Beethoven's influence was infinitely more direct. He wrote the new rules, and his music set the standard against which composers for the next two centuries would measure their work.

In the footsteps of these two came a new generation of musical heroes. The political and economic upheavals of the 18th century produced the world in which they lived, but their vision was their own. This book is about six people who were at the heart of that new generation. They were called *romantics*, and the music they created was radically different from anything that had come before.

WHO WERE THE ROMANTICS?

Modern listeners loosely refer to all serious music, especially anything composed before 1920, as *classical* music. Bach, Beethoven and Brahms, the venerable old "Three B's," are combined, in alphabetical order, under the *classical* sign in music stores. But it's not nearly as simple as that. The music we generally call *classical* was composed over a period of more than 300 years, and includes wildly different styles, traditions and cultures.

For simplicity's sake, we can group this period of European music into three styles: The *baroque* music of the 17th century, whose most famous composer was Johann Sebastian Bach; the *classical* music of 18th century composers such as Wolfgang Amadeus Mozart and Joseph Haydn; and in the 19th century, *romantic* music, created by people like Robert Schumann and performed by the new virtuosi Clara Schumann and Franz Liszt.

Romantic music is not as simple to define as some of the earlier types, because it wasn't taught in a certain school or defined by a specific set of rules. There were as many different styles of romantic music as there were romantic musicians. Through the century, it grew to include the more traditional forms of Johannes Brahms and the radical ideas of Richard Wagner.

It is tempting to assume romantic music got its name from the prodigious love lives of its composers and performers. Actually, the words romantic and romanticism come from the French word *romance*, a narrative poem of the Middle Ages. Usually written in a Romance language (descended from ancient Rome) the stories dealt with grand, epic events. Romantics of the late 18th and early 19th century adopted the name because it called back to an ancient history they admired and wished to emulate. Romantics preached a "return of Nature" and a fascination with the supernatural. They believed they had found a dramatic new way of looking at the world.

CLASSICAL VERSUS ROMANTIC

Philosophers have long identified two contrasting sets of characteristics that are always at war within the human spirit: the struggle between intellect and sentiment; between stern fact and the poet's imagination; scientific method, practicality, symmetry and logic versus the world of sensation, emotion and love. Philosopher's shorthand for these two opposing qualities are *classical* and *romantic*. Politicians give different names to the same concepts: to the monarchist, it is law and order versus anarchy; to the revolutionary, it is dictatorship versus democracy.

Classicism believed that rules for art could be defined and should be followed. In classical music, rules of harmony and composition were not supposed to be limitations, they were designed to stimulate creativity by focusing attention on a carefully controlled set of variables. Romantics believed that true artistic greatness could be achieved only by giving free rein to spontaneous impulse. Logic and reason were replaced with emotional extremes and outbursts of passion. In the 19th century the romantic style swept across Europe.

THE WORLD LOOKED DIFFERENT

Change began a generation earlier when revolutionary French thinker Jean-Jacques Rousseau promoted a new philosophy of personal liberty. He taught freedom from domination by the church or the crown, freedom from ignorance and freedom from tradition. Politically, he declared that the social contract between the government and the governed justified rebellion if the sovereign failed to satisfy the people. American rebels couldn't have agreed more. Thomas Jefferson borrowed heavily from

Rousseau when he spelled out the American belief that governments "derive their just powers from the consent of the government."

The same ideal had strong appeal to Europeans caught up in the ineffective bureaucracies and poor government of the old regime and its nobility. July 14, 1789, celebrated as the beginning of the French revolution, was only the first in a series of dramatic upheavals that shook the French government and climaxed in a coup d'état by Napoleon Bonapart.

THE GENERAL WHO REDREW THE MAP OF EUROPE

Napoleon was an ambitious young general who carefully engineered his rise to power—until he crowned himself Emperor in 1804. History looks back on Napoleon as a tyrant with an insatiable appetite for military conquest. But to the young, European idealists who desperately wanted democracy, Napoleon was a great hero. The French army, which had proved so essential in helping the American rebels defeat England, was expected to act as liberators, not conquerors, in their march across Europe. From 1799 until 1812, Napoleon redrew the map of Europe using his own remarkable blend of military conquest and political intrigue to disrupt all the old alliances. And everywhere he went he left behind political unrest and revolutionary fervor. A coalition of European powers ultimately defeated Napoleon in a series of major battles, but the effects of this revolutionary upheaval could not be removed. Liberal, democratic ideals remained alive, especially among educated people of the middle class. In 1830 and again in 1848-49, popular uprisings challenged authority across Europe.

WHO PAID THE BILLS?

Power and wealth were shifting from old nobility to a new *bourgeois* or middle class. In the old days, the only way to become rich was to be born that way. Wealth was inherited through land and property. There were now a hundred ways to get rich in trade, manufacturing and commerce. Changes in the social order directly affected the place of musicians in the world. The patronage system allowed musicians to work directly for those most able to pay—the church and the nobility. Patronage was essential because music is notoriously time-consuming to create and expensive to perform. But after the revolution, noble patrons were out of power and no longer offered secure positions and valuable patronage. Composers and performers had to find new ways to earn their living.

Romantic musicians found new ways. They toured from city to city, performing before paying audiences of middle class music lovers. They distributed their works through the new music publishing houses and collected royalties. They cultivated the approval of the public—but at the same time, they took their new responsibilities as independent artists very seriously.

Artists began to see themselves as leaders and molders of public taste, rather than mere entertainers who followed public whim—artists who were encouraged to view themselves as heroes, idols and leaders, as geniuses deserving special privileges and outside the norms of behavior. Circumstances had never before allowed composers to defy convention or flout their employer/ princes, but now it was possible to talk back to one's patrons or ride roughshod over the princely class. After the revolution, it was possible for a composer to survive in spite of—or perhaps because of—eccentric behavior.

BEETHOVEN—THE FIRST ROMANTIC

His music was rooted firmly in the classics, but Beethoven was also the first romantic musician. Throughout the course of his career, Beethoven's music changed and grew, clearly reflecting the new romantic style. And his life story shows the dramatic changes that musicians of the era had to survive.

When he moved to Vienna in 1794, Beethoven's music was strictly contained within the discipline of classical forms. His early piano compositions, filled as they were with brilliant music ideas, still echoed earlier styles. But with the turn of the century, his music began to change. The work which we now know as the *Moonlight Sonata*, written in 1801, was originally titled *Sonata quasi una fantasia*—like a fantasy. A fantasy is the prototype romantic musical form. In it, the composer's imagination controls everything, and conventional structures take second place. The *Moonlight* doesn't stray far from the standard sonata form, but the power of Beethoven's imagination is clear.

For the next 25 years Beethoven's musical imagination dominated every form in which he worked, and his music became unquestionably romantic. Its lyrical melodies expanded in complex layers of variation. Simple themes were developed into kaleidoscopes of orchestra sound. Symphonies of epic proportion celebrated heroic achievement, while others serenely reflected the joys of nature. All his music was fiery, passionate and filled with emotional drama. It pushed out the edges of classical form, breaking old rules and making new ones for those who would follow. Finally, breaking completely free of the old symphony structure, Beethoven added voice and poetry to the orchestra and created his final, triumphal testament to human brotherhood, the *Ninth Symphony*.

In his life, as in his work, Beethoven was the model romantic. The fictional heroes of romantic literature all seemed to be isolated, ill and failures at love. Beethoven was all of these. Infected with syphilis at an early age, the disease eventually destroyed his hearing and left him isolated in a world of silence. Tormented by loneliness, he was never able to form a lasting relationship with any of the women he loved.

But in practical areas, Beethoven was a great success. His talent was acknowledged early, and by the time he moved to Vienna he had established a financial base solid enough to no longer need a royal patron. Unlike Mozart, who quickly sank into poverty when he lost his patronage, Beethoven mastered the art of earning a living in the competitive musical marketplace of Vienna.

IN BEETHOVEN'S FOOTSTEPS

Many romantic musicians followed in Beethoven's footsteps. They lived and worked near each other, performed in the same concert halls, mingled in the same salons and fought about music, politics and love. This book is about six of the most fascinating musicians of that time, all of whom could be called romantics, though their ideals were very different.

The first trio of musicians built on an idealistic tradition that demanded discipline and self-sacrifice. All three suffered great personal tragedies, but found strength and liberation in their music.

The second trio was drawn to romanticism's darker side. They indulged in artistic license and celebrated a cult of personality. In a way, these three became prisoners of their celebrity, and in turn, they used music as a weapon to manipulate others.

All six made significant contributions to the music of their century—and ours. Understanding their lives will give a new perspective on the musical legacies they left behind.

THE
FIRST
TRIO

CLARA WIECK SCHUMANN
ROBERT SCHUMANN
JOHANNES BRAHMS

MUSIC'S CHILDREN

*People compose for many reasons: to become im-
mortal; because the piano happens to be open; to
become a millionaire; because of the praise of a
friend; or because they have looked into a pair of
beautiful eyes...*

—Robert Schumann

O n a mild March evening in 1828, a careful observer would have discovered a sign—hand-lettered in elaborate German script—hanging on a door one block from the center of Leipzig.

Friedrich Wieck.
Creator and Sole Teacher of the Wieck System of Piano Study.
Instruction in Theory, Harmony, Composition and Counterpoint.
Voice Lessons if Desired.
Pianos of Outstanding Quality for Sale or Rent.
Circulating Library of Sheet Music, Including the World's Greatest Classics.
Consultations by Appointment.

It was the home of Friedrich Wieck and his daughter Clara, and probably the most musical home in a very musical city.

As the evening grew darker and lamps began to appear in the windows of row houses, the door behind the sign opened and the remarkable pair stepped out onto the street.

Wieck was tall and powerful, with a heavy jaw and a bulldog-stubborn scowl on his face. At the age of 43, his head was balding and he brushed what remained of his hair forward in two elaborate wings to cover the sides of his head. He walked rapidly down the street, like a man who knew exactly where he was going. Holding his hand was his eight-year-old daughter, Clara. She was a tiny girl, but her little body was strong and she easily kept up with his brisk walk. She wore a long satin dress with an elaborate lace pinafore, and her eyes were so large they seemed to take up most of her face.

They were on their way to an evening musicale. It was one more opportunity for Wieck to show off his skill as a teacher. Clara was a walking advertisement for his success.

Wieck was determined to make Clara into the most famous concert pianist in Europe. He had made that decision before she was born. Her playing would prove the absolute superiority of his teaching methods and make him a respected man. He was personally creating a child prodigy, following in a well-established tradition of the times begun by Leopold Mozart, the father of Wolfgang Amadeus Mozart.

Herr Mozart was the first, and perhaps worst, of the stage fathers. He dragged his tiny children through the courts of Europe for fun and profit. Unfortunately, his example encouraged hundreds of equally ambitious fathers to look at their children as exploitable resources. Following the Mozart model, baby fingers were set to work on keyboards and violin strings. The 19th century became the age of the would-be prodigy, and many lives were destroyed or distorted in the attempt.

One notable casualty was Ludwig van Beethoven. As a child, his abusive, alcoholic father was determined to make him a musical gold mine. The elder Beethoven beat and bullied the child, who failed as a prodigy. And although his talent survived the rough handling, the lonely, frightened boy became a miserable, isolated and angry man. His music was saved but his humanity was lost in the process.

The child who could survive a prodigy's exhausting, unnatural life—with emotional and musical abilities intact—was rare indeed.

Friedrich Wieck triumphed. Clara became a remarkably skilled pianist at an early age, receiving honors all over Europe. Clara Wieck would go on to become a successful adult performer, but she would pay a heavy price for her prodigy.

Clara was a survivor. She was born with a strong body and a sturdy emotional makeup. Her father, though a cold and manipulative man, gave her excellent training and helped her build a solid career. But the most important gift he gave her was music. The tool he was using to build his own career became the most powerful survival skill Clara had. Music was the focus of her entire life—it gave her strength, support and comfort when no human being could. And each of the major relationships of her life was built around music. Father, husband and lifelong companion would each be united with Clara by a bond of music.

Clara's story begins with her father, because more than most children, she was a creation of her father. With determination and care, he set out to design the perfect child prodigy. He had plenty of practice creating people, because he started by creating himself.

Friedrich Wieck was the classic self-made man. Born into a family with good breeding and bad credit, he became a success through intelligence, ambition and absolutely brazen self-promotion. After receiving a degree in theology, he followed the traditional path of ambitious German university graduates with no money—he became a tutor to a wealthy family.

While working as a tutor, he made up his mind that the teaching of music was his destiny and set out to train himself. A self-taught pianist of only average skill, he was an unlikely person to set himself up as a music teacher. But Wieck studied the rationalists and the most modern education psychologists. He poured over the best of the new music teachers, such as Karl Czerny, who were revolutionizing the way music was taught to children. He borrowed freely from anything he could lay his hands on. From all this material, he created his own course of musical study, and set off to promote it.

In 1814, Friedrich Wieck began accepting piano students in Leipzig. He was well on his way to becoming the self-appointed spokesman for good piano teaching. Now all he needed was someone to help him make his name better known. The fastest way to public acceptance was with performance, but Wieck was not a performer. The next best way was to have one's students perform, and he looked around for the best available vehicle. He found her in 19-year-old Marianne Tromlitz. In 1816, at age 30, Wieck became her music teacher, promoter and husband. He was relentless in pursuit of professional success, and she was an excellent weapon in his assault on the musical establishment.

Marianne did her best to meet his expectations, which were grand indeed. In the seven years of their marriage, she studied piano to perfect her virtuoso technique, ran the household, gave birth to five children, taught advanced voice and piano lessons, and performed as a soprano soloist in such major works as Mozart's Requiem and Beethoven's Mass in C. Every successful performance built Wieck's reputation.

By the time their daughter Clara was born on September 13, 1819, Wieck had established a name as one of Germany's top piano teachers. He had also borrowed money to establish a music and book lending library and set himself up as one of the leading piano sales agents in Leipzig. To promote the sale of pianos, Wieck decided that Marianne needed more public piano performance experience, so in November and December of 1823, she performed the English composer John Field's Second Piano Concerto—while six months pregnant with her son Victor. When Victor was three months old, Marianne took the baby and her eldest daughter Clara home to her father's house and announced her intention to stay there. She'd had enough of Friedrich. He was crude, cruel and had a vicious temper. His ambitions had exhausted her. And, she was in love with his best friend, Adolf Bargiel.

Leaving Wieck must have been an especially difficult decision for her, because under Saxon law children were literally their father's property. If a father chose to punish the wife who left him, it was his prerogative to deny her any contact with her children. Wieck did exactly that. He left the baby with Marianne only until it was weaned and demanded that Clara be returned to him on her fifth birthday. He actually took possession four days before. Wieck needed Clara in order to continue his career plan. It was essential for her education to begin.

Her lessons began the day after her fifth birthday. To make a clean sweep of the household and remove everything that reminded Clara of her mother, Wieck also fired Clara's nanny. This meant that the only two people who had ever shown warmth and caring for Clara were snatched away within the space of a few months.

Clara began to make music, but her voice was silent. She developed a kind of selective deafness. Even before her mother left, Clara had been unable to speak or understand words. She simply stopped being able to hear. She could hear and understand music, but didn't choose to speak. Because she was so quick to understand and imitate the music played for her, it's reasonable to assume that her "deafness" was emotionally caused. The stress of her parents' tense, sometimes violent relationship, followed by the pain of losing both mother and beloved nanny caused her to retreat into silence.

For four years, Wieck remained single and Clara was the center of his world—the focus of all his ambitions. She progressed through his carefully disciplined series of studies, exercises and educational programs. Wieck's musical intentions, at least, were excellent. He didn't want to make her a machine or a trained monkey. He was trying to develop in this already talented child a real musical sensitivity. Her schedule at age six included three hours of tutoring, a one hour piano lesson from her father, two hours of practice, and a long walk for fresh air and exercise. She continued the habit of walking one or two hours each day for her whole life, and gave exercise the credit for her excellent health and stamina. Except for six months at a primary school when she was with other children, she was taught at home. Gradually, she gained the use of speech.

Music was the family's entire life—they ate, breathed and slept music. Clara focused her complete attention on her father and her music. She progressed rapidly in her music and became a calm, well-behaved child who was obsessively devoted to her father. Wieck was never cruel to Clara, who was the goose getting ready to lay the golden egg. Instead, he focused his abuse on her two brothers, Alwin and Gustav. Physical and emotional cruelty toward them were an everyday part of life in the Wieck household.

Although Clara was never physically harmed, she was subjected to a much more subtle and effective kind of abuse. Her father's affections were completely and absolutely tied to her musical progress, and she was never loved for herself, only for her performance. If she performed properly, she was rewarded with praise. If she was lazy in her practice or did not meet his high musical standards, she was punished with immediate loss of her father's affection—and with separation from her beloved piano. With such powerful emotional control, and with her exceptional natural gift for music, Clara progressed rapidly. But her "deafness" didn't fully disappear until she was eight, when she began to speak normally.

Clara started performing at private musical evenings in the Wieck home when she was six, and by the spring of 1828 she was performing regularly at informal musical entertainments in the homes of friends.

On that particular evening in March, her father was taking her to the home of Dr. E.A. Carus and his beautiful wife Agnes. Dr. Carus had been the director of an insane asylum, and was now teaching at Leipzig University. Since their arrival in Leipzig from Zwickau, amateur and professional musicians enjoyed meeting in the Carus home for evenings of music and conversation. Their musicales weren't unusual in this city. Leipzig was devoted to music.

Leipzig was a successful commercial trading center with a population of more than 40,000 people, and the new middle class of Leipzig believed that music belonged to the people—not just to the wealthy nobility or royalty. The merchants and tradesmen of Leipzig supported a wide variety of public music.

Since 1763, Leipzigers had gathered together and supported subscription concerts held in their famous Gewandhaus concert hall. St. Thomas Church, just off the square, was the old home of Johann Sebastian Bach, whom the folks of Leipzig remembered affectionately as "Old Bach." Fine teachers and the most promising students were drawn from all over Europe to the University of Leipzig. The city also boasted a professional opera and over a dozen choral societies.

But perhaps its most valuable musical resource was the world-famous music publishing house, Breitkopf & Härtel. In a world where all music had to be laboriously copied by hand, only the very rich could afford new music. The ability to print music inexpensively and in large quantities changed the whole process of how new music was distributed and how musicians were paid.

Bernhard Breitkopf opened the publishing house in 1719. In 1754 he and his son introduced state-of-the-art technology—moveable type. Moveable type was as revolutionary in music publishing as it was to Guttenberg's first Bible. It made mass distribution possible. Composers who wanted to escape from the economic tyranny of their noble patrons now had a new source of income. To them, sales of sheet music meant independence and artistic freedom. And when music became cheap enough for amateurs to buy and learn, interest in making music absolutely boomed. Everyone became a musician—and nowhere more than in Leipzig.

Walking down the streets of Leipzig on any afternoon, one could hear music coming from many windows. Music was performed often in public, but it was performed even more frequently in the home. Every young person with any discernable talent (and many without it) studied an instrument. Every home that could possibly afford one boasted a pianoforte. The most important evening's entertainment in many Leipzig front parlors was the gathering of friends to play music together. The music they played may not have been very good, in composition or in execution, but it was played with enthusiasm and real affection.

The music played tonight would be much better than the average.

When the pair arrived at the Carus home, the evening's musical entertainments were already underway. The parlor was brightly lit with lamps and candles and guests sat quietly, listening to the hostess's beautiful soprano voice singing a romantic song by Franz Schubert. The young composer's music had only recently arrived from Vienna, and his haunting melodies were extremely popular in Leipzig.

At the piano accompanying Mrs. Carus was a young man Clara had never met. His long, wavy hair fell down over his forehead as he bent over the keyboard. When he looked up at the music, his deep blue eyes caught the light from the candle on the piano. Clara thought he was the most beautiful boy she had ever seen. She especially liked the dimple in his chin.

When the song finished, the young man played a short sonata. Wieck looked down at Clara and frowned. She caught his expression and understood its meaning—the playing really wasn't technically good. But it had great feeling and emotion. Then, someone from across the room said, "Robert, why don't you improvise something?"

The boy's eyes became dreamy and he paused for a moment in complete silence. He pursed his lips as if he were going to whistle a silent tune and smiled to himself. Then he began to play a theme and variations unlike any Clara had ever heard. The notes were filled with longing and sweetness and a passion she didn't understand. When he finished, the listeners burst into applause. He tugged at his ear in embarrassment and quickly left the piano.

Clara went to the keyboard to play her pieces. She performed a string trio with two violinists her father had asked to attend. Then she played a difficult Mozart sonata. Her playing, as always, was strong, subtle and self-assured. It was surprisingly mature for a girl so young and so small. Everyone in the Carus home already knew of her great skill and they were an appreciative audience, calling her back to the keyboard two more times with applause and good-natured cheers. Each encore was a pleasure for her. She had already learned to love the respect of an audience, and she looked forward to playing in public. Throughout her life, she always felt most powerful when she was on stage in front of a piano. There, she was in control.

When she finished playing, Clara searched through the crowd to find her father—and to see if she could find the beautiful young man with the dreamy eyes and the dimple in his chin. When she found him, he was talking to her father.

"Clara," said Wieck, "this is Herr Robert Schumann of Zwickau. He will be attending the University next term. He says he has come to study law, but I think he really wants to take piano lessons from me. What do you think, is there any hope for him?"

"I like your playing, Mr. Schumann," Clara answered solemnly, "but I think you shall also be a very good composer." Twenty years later, all he could remember of their first meeting was a single thought; her eyes really were much too big.

A ROMANTIC COMING OF AGE

I do not love the men whose lives are not in harmony with their works.

—Florestan

Herr Robert Schumann's apartment in Leipzig was comfortable—almost luxurious. Two large rooms were filled with fine furniture and a huge grand piano looked out over a gracious garden. In his study, a great mahogany desk was stacked with correspondence and diaries. Over the desk hung portraits of the romantic writer Jean Paul Richter, Schumann's late father August and the Emperor Napoleon.

On this night in 1828 the house was filled with the sounds of music and of champagne corks popping. At the piano sat Schumann, his shirt sleeves rolled up, a cigar clenched between his teeth and a glass of champagne perched on the edge of the keyboard. He and two other Leipzig University students were playing a loud and very enthusiastic version of Schubert's E Flat Trio to an appreciative audience of Robert's guests. Among the listeners, in a rare moment of champagne-induced good cheer, was Robert's new piano teacher, Friedrich Wieck.

This was the one place in Leipzig where Robert felt completely happy. He hated the university and he thoroughly disliked the violent, anti-intellectual atmosphere of the student clubs and dueling societies. Instead of attending classes, Robert spent his time playing the piano, walking in the country, studying with Herr Wieck, reading novels, drinking good Bavarian beer and writing poetry. Why was this most unwilling student in Leipzig?

Because his mother wanted him to be, and he hadn't yet found a way to change her mind without losing his allowance.

Robert Schumann was born on June 8, 1810 in the small Saxon town of Zwickau. He was the youngest of five children and his mother's darling.

Schumann's father, August Gottlob Schumann, was a remarkably talented man. The son of a poor country cleric, August worked his way through Leipzig University as a clerk in a book store, where he fell in love with the daughter of the owner, Johanna Christiane Schnabel. Johanna's father said August was too poor to be a suitable husband, so August came up with a remarkable plan. He went home and wrote seven books in the next 18 months. It was an amazing feat, and even more amazingly, he found a publisher for all seven and was paid one thousand thalers for his work, equivalent to about $20,000 in 1990 dollars. It was a huge sum for a young man with no family connections and no capital.

The thousand thalers opened the door to Johanna's affections, but it didn't completely win over her father. The old man insisted that August open a grocery store in order to support her. In spite of the thousand thalers, the literary arts still didn't strike Johanna's father as stable enough. August opened the store and married the girl, but his heart wasn't in the grocery business. As soon as they were married, he left Johanna to run the store and retired to the back room to write more books. Four years later, he abandoned the grocery and began a publishing house. Specializing in inexpensive German editions of international classics, the business prospered and built up a small but solid personal fortune.

August was a man of great ambition and drive, but he had what was known in those times as a "nervous condition," alternating between periods of deeply withdrawn, antisocial behavior and exhausting months of 24-hour work. He was fond of his young son, but saw him only on rare occasions as a child. By the time Robert was 14, his father's mental health had deteriorated so badly that he saw almost no one, even within the family. Raising the boy was left mostly to his mother.

Although Johanna Schumann provided the solid surroundings that were expected of a good German hausfrau, she suffered from periods of severe depression. Her marriage to August was not happy, and they were estranged under the same roof for many years.

This is how an anonymous Victorian writer described Robert's mother:

> *In later years she fell into an exaggerated state of romance and sentimentalism, united with sudden and violent passions, and an inclination to singularity, to which conjugal difference may have contributed.*

In modern translation, that means that Johanna Schumann was an unpleasant woman in a miserable marriage who totally lost contact with reality as she grew older.

But no matter how difficult Johanna may have appeared to anyone else, she was the first and largest love of Robert's life. They remained intimate and dependent on each other until the day she died.

A gifted student, Robert had what his mother liked to call leadership qualities—he was ambitious, likeable and bossy. He began taking music lessons before he was eight from a Zwickau high school teacher named Kuntzsch. Not a world-class teacher, Kuntzsch still encouraged the boy's love of music and taught him the basics. Robert began composing little dances, and more importantly, he developed a real talent for improvising. By the age of eight, he was able to create small pieces that sketched characters— comic musical caricatures that were so accurate they usually prompted loud laughter from the parlor audience.

He also loved to write and produce plays, which he performed on a small stage his father had hired a carpenter to build. Robert's father was happy to encourage his literary ambitions, including him in the family publishing business. He also encouraged his musical interests. In a rare outing together, Papa took the boy to see the famous pianist Ignatz Moscheles, who performed in Carlsbad when Robert was nine. Moscheles' music filled Robert with passionate ambition to be a great musician.

The next year, Robert struck up an acquaintance with the son of the regimental band leader. They played four hand-works of Haydn, Mozart and the newest Beethoven symphonies. Robert's father brought him a magnificent Steck grand piano from Vienna, and used his position as a publisher to gather up a valuable library of music for the boys to work from. Robert performed around town and gained a reputation as a prodigy.

In his father's office, Robert found a complete orchestral score that had probably been sent to the publisher by mistake. With typical enthusiasm, he gathered up every friend he had with any musical competence and began an orchestra. It included two violins, two flutes, a clarinet and two horns. There were important gaps in instrumentation and in talent, but Robert was sure he could make up for all of those, filling in anything that was missing on the piano. By the time he was twelve, Robert had made the orchestra a regular event, performing anything he could get his hands on, often with his father as the only audience. His mother would not attend, calling music "the breadless art" and not a suitable occupation for any well-brought-up young man.

Watching all this ambitious musical activity, Robert's Papa was convinced his son had a future in music. Mama was not.

Johanna Schumann was not a woman of musical vision. It's not hard to imagine her voice in the parlor screaming, "Do you think Mozart's mother wanted him to be a musician? Remember how he suffered, how miserable his poor wife must have been? My darling little Robert must have a better life, he must have a respectable job, nothing lower-class like music."

For a while, Papa prevailed, even going so far as writing the great composer Carl Maria von Weber and asking him to supervise the boy's musical education. But Weber's death when Robert was 16 ended any possibility of a musical apprenticeship. A few months later, when Schumann's father died, all hope of studying music was gone. If Papa had encouraged the boy's artistic ambitions, Mama would have none of it. She wanted him to study law.

It would be hard to imagine a more unlikely profession for a dreamy young man who was subject to dramatic mood swings, but she was determined. One wonders why Robert gave in and agreed to study at the University of Leipzig. Probably, he never had any intention of taking the course seriously, and humoring Mama was easier than making a scene. But in truth, Schumann wasn't completely dedicated to music either; his interests were evenly divided between poetry, music and drinking champagne. Until he had made up his mind for certain, it would be easier just to collect the income from his small inheritance, skip classes and have a good time. Mama may have appeared determined, but Robert always managed to win eventually. He was very good at getting his own way.

And so, in the spring of 1828, after graduating with honors from high school, and a good deal of preliminary fooling around, Robert Schumann came to Leipzig and the University. He found a roommate, an old friend from Zwickau, and made a new friend, Gilbert Rosen. Robert and Gilbert immediately became comrades, but Gilbert was leaving soon to study at Heidelberg University. Robert took him home for two weeks to attend his brother Julius' wedding. Then they headed off together for adventures. During the vacation they visited the home of Robert's boyhood literary hero Jean Paul in Bayreuth. Staying with friends in Augsburg, Robert wangled an introduction to the world-famous poet Heinrich Heine, who lived in Munich.

Heine's home was luxurious, hung with original paintings by Munich's leading artists. He criticized Robert for studying law when he should be seeking after truth and beauty. Heine himself had studied law but never practiced, though he neglected to mention that his own gracious lifestyle was made possible by the support of a generous, rich uncle. Schumann would someday guarantee the immortality of Heine's poem's by setting them to music in the most beautiful of all German songs.

The two boys drank lots of beer, did a little wenching and returned to Leipzig after a short visit with Robert's mother. It was time to go to school.

University life was lonely and frustrating. The only bright spot in his life was his relationship with the Wieck family. He spent many hours in their parlor, taking lessons, playing duets with Clara and reading books from Wieck's large library. He rarely, if ever, studied law. But he did immediately discover where all the prettiest girls in Leipzig took their afternoon walks, where the best beer was served—and most importantly, where the best music was being made.

After a year in Leipzig, Robert decided to change Universities and study in Heidelberg. In his letter to his mother, asking permission to make the change, Robert claimed the move would allow him to study with the great law professor Anton Friedrich Justus Thibaut. As usual in his dealings with his mother, he was telling only part of the truth. Thibaut was a law professor, but his real love was music. Robert wanted to join the professor's musical circle, and that's just what he did. After a little resistance, his mother agreed.

Professor Thibaut's great house in the city of Heidelberg was a bee hive of musical activity. Each Friday evening, more than 70 musicians would gather around his piano to practice Handel oratorios. Thibaut's great head of white hair was always at the center of the group, accompanying the musicians with more passion than skill, so moved by the beauty of the music that tears would roll down his cheeks. Through Thibaut, Robert was introduced into the city's musical circles and soon became the new musical darling of Heidelberg. Every night was filled with music and social events: Monday at the musical society, Tuesday at Professor Mittermayer's, Thursdays at a brilliant gathering of English ladies, Friday at Thibaut's and Saturday at the home of the widowed Grand Duchess Stephanie, who was enchanted with the young man's skills at the piano and on the dance floor.

The only thing he did not have time to do was study law. There is no evidence that he ever attended more than a few classes at the University. His major occupations were practicing the piano and writing home for money.

Schumann polished his literary technique in dozens of begging letters to his mother, brothers, sisters-in-law and the legal guardian who watched over his investments. He was absolutely relentless in his requests for additions to his allowance. "Send as much as you can, as quick as you can," was a common request, most often granted. At this point in his life, the young spendthrift was absolutely incapable of living within his means.

After a year in Heidelberg, the myth of law school couldn't last much longer. In one last, vain attempt to catch up, he signed up for a short, intensive study course, but it was rapidly becoming obvious to Robert that he would never pass his examinations. The time finally came to declare his intentions to his mother.

At 5 p.m. on July 30 of 1830, Robert sat down and wrote an impassioned letter to his mother:

> *In Leipzig I lived carelessly without a plan of life. I dreamed and loafed, and, strictly speaking, accomplished nothing. Here I have worked more, but, both there and here, have become more and more closely attached to music. Now I stand at the crossways, and am startled at the question—whither? If I follow my genius it directs me to music—I believe, the right way. But in truth—do not take it amiss, I say it only lovingly and gently—it always seemed to me as if you obstructed my way. You had, of course, your good motherly reasons, which I understand very well, and which you and I called "precarious future and uncertain bread." What next? There can be no more tormenting thought for a man than an unhappy, lifeless, empty future of his own preparing.*

His mother agreed that he could quit school and study with Wieck, who acknowledged his talent and promised to make him a great virtuoso piano player in three years. Robert was 20 years old, late in life to make a commitment to music. But he had declared himself and there was no turning back.

In an earlier era, when children's musical destinies were decided early and their teaching begun at age six or seven, the idea of a young man choosing music as a career at age 20 would have seemed absurd. Of course many children, like Clara Schumann and Franz Liszt, were still being put to work early. But in this new romantic era, some talents were discovered late. The idea of a young man becoming a composer without formal training suited the romantic sensibility. Whatever he lacked in traditional knowledge, he could surely make up in emotional intensity. At least that was the idea Robert Schumann shared with another young man from his neighborhood, Richard Wagner. Both composers regretted their lack of technical skills at some time during their careers, but their independence from the classical tradition also gave them freedom to be musically inventive, and their music reflects that freedom.

Robert Schumann moved back to Leipzig and moved into the Wieck home as a lodger. As he sat in the library of the Wieck home, deeply engrossed in studying an orchestral score, he suddenly became aware of someone watching him. In front of him stood his young friend Clara, staring at him with a grave expression. Now twelve years old, Clara's face was growing into her eyes, and she was becoming more mature every day. The serious responsibilities of her growing performing career made her seem older than her age, and she never giggled or made jokes. Only Robert could bring her to laughter with his fantastic imaginary stories and games of hide and seek.

"What do you want, Klärich?" he asked.

"Nothing. I was just studying your face."

Wieck put Schumann on a demanding series of exercises and suggested he study theory and composition with the Cantor of St. Thomas School, Bach's old place of employment. Robert instead chose to work with Heinrich

Dorn, the young musical director of the Leipzig opera. For less than a year, he studied with Dorn. It was the only formal composition training he would ever receive. Throughout 1831, he continued to diligently study the piano and work on his compositions.

Wieck had promised to make Robert a virtuoso, but the teacher was often too wrapped up in managing his daughter's career to spend much time teaching Robert. That was all right with his student. He already doubted whether his shyness and introspection would ever allow him to be a very good performer. His deepest love was for composition. So he took long walks with Clara, told ghost stories to her brothers and worked on his music.

By the fall of 1832, he had written a Piano Sonata in B minor, the first movement of a symphony and his first important composition, *Papillons. Papillons* is a series of little dances inspired by a Jean Paul poem about butterflies. This set of short piano pieces was held together by a single idea—butterflies fluttering in the wide glorious world of spring. The idea of joining many small musical scenes together to create a larger image was new with Schumann, and he was to use it again in other piano works. *Papillons* was accepted for publication in January of 1832, and Schumann wrote his mother:

> *Spring itself stands outside the door and gazes at me—a child with heavenly blue eyes—and now I begin to comprehend my own existence.*

Clara's career was beginning to blossom too. She made her solo debut at the Gewandhaus to rave reviews and published a set of four *Polonaises*. At that time, all performers were expected to include a certain number of original compositions or improvisations in each concert. Clara was no exception. Her first compositions were delicate, graceful and lyrical. She and Schumann often discussed the development of their works, sharing musical ideas and solving problems of theory. But soon that daily intimacy would have to end. Wieck had determined that Clara, who was now a masterly performer, was ready for the big time. To prepare the way for her first concert tour, Wieck set out on a promotional trip. He decided that the tour would end in Paris, so he traced the entire route himself first, arranging concerts whenever possible, or introducing himself to local musical dignitaries in hopes of getting their help with Clara's career.

One of his most important stops was a visit to the ailing Beethoven. Without an introduction or any idea of how he was going to get in the front door, Wieck simply presented himself on the old man's doorstep and asked to be let in. It was a classic example of his fearless self-promotion, and it worked. He was granted a brief, uncomfortable audience and left with the composer's autograph. In September of 1831, the tour began with a visit to the legendary poet-philosopher Johann Wolfgang von Goethe. It had been a struggle for Wieck to arrange the meeting. He had begged, pestered and harassed everyone in Weimar who might possibly know Goethe, until someone finally relented and arranged a meeting. The old man, who had a well-known fondness for lovely young girls, was happy to meet Clara. He asked her to sit beside him on the sofa, asked her a few questions about herself and then gave her permission to play. When the piano stool was too low, 83-year-old Goethe fetched a pillow and settled her on the stool. She played a flashy, bravura piece guaranteed to impress a non-musician, and he was indeed impressed. When the traveling pair left, Wieck was clutching a portrait and a note inscribed "For the gifted artist Clara Wieck." It was just the sort of tool he could use to leverage their way into other concert halls.

In Weimar, Clara performed at court and received excellent reviews. Their long journey continued through Erfurt, Arnstadt and Gotha. In some towns she played in good concert halls with well-tuned pianos and receptive audiences. Just as often, at least one of those things was lacking. Clara's job was to play her best every day, regardless of the circumstances. Wieck's responsibility was to make the proper contacts, rent the halls, try to repair the ancient pianos, publicize the concert and collect the money at the door. He added extra income by selling portraits of Clara to concert-goers as they left the auditorium. All of the money went into his own account. Clara was given only enough for candy and postage.

Clara studied everything her father did and acquired an excellent practical education in concert management, which she put to use herself throughout her whole career.

Her performances received excellent reviews wherever she played, and Clara always enjoyed playing. The exhausting travel schedule never seemed to tire her and her performances were consistently strong, even under difficult conditions.

At the age of 14, Clara was still a thin-faced girl with a small, pointed chin and enormous dark eyes. For concerts, she wore her hair swept onto the top of her head in a chignon, long dangling earrings and elaborate white gowns designed in the latest Paris styles.

A letter, allegedly written by the poet Heine, described Clara during her Paris stay:

> *At first glance Clara seems to be a quite lovable 13-year-old girl...and one thinks no more about it—but observed more closely, everything seems quite different! The delicate, pretty little face with the somewhat strangely shaped eyes, the friendly mouth with the touch of sentiment that now and then draws up in a some-*

*what mocking or wistful way, particularly when
she answers. And the mixture of grace and
carelessness in her movements—not studied,
but it goes far beyond one of her years. All this—
I confess it openly—stirred a quite peculiar feeling in me when I saw it. I know of no better way
to describe it except as "an echo of Clara's
mocking-painful" smile. It seems as though the
child could tell a long story, a story woven out of
joy and pain—and yet—what does she know?
Music.*

Paris was already crowded with piano players when
they arrived. The brilliant Polish composer, Fryderyk
Chopin was there, but he couldn't get anyone to listen to
him except Clara. A handsome young man with an angelic
mass of fair curly hair and agreeable manners, Chopin was
something of a dandy—as concerned about his hair, his
clothes and his gloves as he was about his piano
technique. He made a strong impression on the young
Clara, though she confessed it was more for his glorious
music than his manners. The young Felix Mendelssohn
was making friends and winning supporters too, while
Franz Liszt created a major sensation and left the ladies
swooning in the aisles. Audiences were spread thin, and
although Clara's playing was excellent, the crowds were
small. It was time to go home.

Robert Schumann no longer lived in the Wieck
home. He had rented a small apartment a few blocks
away. When Clara returned home from Paris, he was one
of her first visitors. In his hand was a copy of his first
published work, *Papillons.* And he had disheartening
news about his piano studies.

"I have suffered a mysterious injury to the fingers of
my right hand," he said. "They are painful and I have
trouble controlling them. I have been to every sort of

doctor, even a few quacks, but no treatment seems to help. I'm forced to admit that I will never be a great performer like you are, so I am devoting myself entirely to composition. You, Clara, will have to be my right hand."

She immediately began learning the *Papillons,* eventually adding them to her concert repertoire. From that time forward, Clara was always the first to perform his piano works.

In November of 1832, the following advertisement appeared in the Zwickau newspaper:

CLARA WIECK

The celebrated 13-year-old pianoforte virtuosa will give with her father, Herr Wieck, a great pianoforte concert in the hall of the (Zwickau) Gewandhaus, with the co-operation of the Choral Society. Herr Schumann will at the same time produce some movements of his first Symphony. Price of admission, six groschen per person.

The first public performance of Robert's work was to be in his hometown, and the Wiecks stayed with his family while they were in Zwickau. Robert's first attempt at a symphony was performed badly by a badly rehearsed orchestra—although it probably wasn't written very well either. No record of it exists today because he completely rewrote the work. But Clara's performance was, as usual, remarkable. The audiences were impressed and so was Frau Schumann. She was also charmed by the young woman's natural, unaffected character and sweet disposition.

One snowy November night, Frau Schumann and Clara were standing by the window of the Schumann's upstairs sitting room. Looking out the window onto Zwickau's town square, they saw Robert, coming home from the Gewandhaus rehearsals. He looked up at them, smiled and waved. Frau Schumann saw the warm response in Clara's face and smiled. "Someday," she said, "you must marry my Robert."

After the concert, the Wiecks went home, but Robert stayed behind with his mother for a few months. When he returned to Leipzig in March of 1833, he brought with him an important discovery—new compositions by Chopin. Each day, Robert and Clara went for walks together and then returned to the Wieck piano to play Chopin. Both were enthusiastic about the new works and Clara was already performing them in her concerts. Chopin was a poet at the keyboard, writing almost exclusively for the piano. He experimented with new and subtle harmonies, and his work thrilled Robert and Clara. The critics of his time called his music "barbaric, wild and dissonant," but the new ideas he introduced sounded bold, rich and exuberant to the young romantics. His compositions enlarged the capabilities of the piano and raised the expectations of anyone who listened to them in performance. Robert wrote an enthusiastic essay about Chopin and sent it out to publishers.

Schumann's opinions on music were passionate and he was frustrated for lack of a place to publish his writing about music. He wasn't the only one. All across Europe, young composers found it virtually impossible to get any notice at all from the established music press. Few of the periodicals of the day would condescend to reviewing any new compositions, and many of the old-line writers were outrageously prejudiced in their views. There was no attempt to write objective or unbiased information on new music, and most critics unashamedly promoted or destroyed strictly on the basis of their personal friendships or the economic demands of music publishers.

This lack of an avenue to share new musical information was even more important to Robert, who knew his
own compositions would never reach a wider audience
without publicity. Drawing on his experience working in
his father's publishing house, Robert decided to start his
own magazine. This is how he described its beginnings:

> *In Leipzig toward the end of 1833 a few*
> *musicians, mostly young men, met as though by*
> *accident every evening. What brought them*
> *together chiefly was their pleasure in each other's*
> *company; also their desire to discuss the art*
> *which was the meat and drink of life to them,*
> *music. The musical situation in Germany at the*
> *moment was anything but inspiring. Rossini*
> *reigned in the opera-houses, and nothing was to*
> *be heard on the pianoforte save Herz and Huen-*
> *ten. Yet merely a few years had passed since*
> *Beethoven, C.M. von Weber and Franz Schubert*
> *had lived among us.*
>
> *It is true that Mendelssohn's star was*
> *rising and wondrous tales were told of a Pole*
> *named Chopin. But neither of these composers*
> *had as yet begun to exert his future far-reaching*
> *influence. So on a day the following idea came*
> *to these musical young hot-heads: "Let us not be*
> *mere spectators! Let us lend a hand ourselves for*
> *the glory of things! Let us bring the poetry of our*
> *art into honor once again!"*

Thus the first pages of a new musical magazine called
the *Neue Zeitschrift für Musik* (*New Journal for Music*)
saw the light.

The group put together their savings, arranged for
loans to finance the rest and found a publisher. Robert, as
the most powerful of the personalities, and the hardest

working, became the *New Journal's* leading voice and eventually its sole editor. The first edition appeared on April 3, 1834. He continued to publish the paper twice a week for 10 years, until the demands of his career and then his growing illness forced him to hand over the management to others.

The articles and reviews contained in the *New Journal* reflected Schumann's own personal vision, although he accepted contributions from many different writers. The form was independent, revolutionary, and often quite funny.

One dramatically different journalistic technique Schumann used was to present major articles as discussions between members of an imaginary club called the Davidsbündler.

Schumann described them this way:

> *Here I must mention another society, a more secret one, since it never existed anywhere save in the imagination of its founder: that of the Davidsbündler. In view of the desirability of dramatizing the different points of view from which works of art may be discussed, it seemed opportune to invent antithetic artist-characters to whom these different views might be ascribed. The most important of these characters were Florestan and Eusebius: between them as a mediator stood Master Raro. Like a scarlet thread this society of Davidsbündler ran through the entire journal, mingling "Truth" and "Poetry" in humorous fashion. The public enjoyed these likable fellows.*

Usually translated as Davidites, the Davidsbündler name might be more accurately translated as David's Bunch. It wouldn't be that wrong to imagine them as a wild bunch of 19th-century musicians hanging around street corners wearing leather jackets. The David in question was the young David of the Bible, who made such an impression on the Philistines by killing their big hero, Goliath. The target of this group was the modern German Philistines who Schumann felt were killing all creativity in modern music. The Philistines were "everything stuffy, narrow, prejudiced, reactionary," that Schumann hated. He battled them his whole life.

Fictional members of the club, such as the volatile Florestan and the thoughtful Eusebius, were listed as contributors on the title page of the *New Journal.* Their names were often attached to articles, as were other fictional members of the Davidsbündler. Other articles were signed simply with numbers. The result of all this whimsy and confusion was great freedom of expression for all the writers. Anonymity became the key to honesty, especially since Schumann was quite willing to take the heat for anything published in the *New Journal.*

It's important to remember that in this culture, music was a critical part of everyday life. Discussing a new symphony in 19th-century Leipzig would arouse passions as intense as asking a cab driver about the Cubs in 20th-century Chicago. What's more, the composers and performers were not a large number of people scattered across great geographic areas. They were a small, almost incestuous group, tied together by their loves and hatreds, and were bound to come in contact again and again. The *New Journal* allowed music critics the freedom to offer opinions, free from the fear of a punch in the nose.

Many of Schumann's reviews were written as imaginary dialogs between members of the Davidsbündler. Using a dialog between fictional characters as a technique for expressing differing points of view wasn't new. Plato did it, and the method was used by a number of Robert's favorite Romantic writers, such as E.T.A. Hoffman and Jean Paul. The technique especially appealed to Schumann because his own internal dialogues were extremely lively, and his own identity seemed—even to him—to be a little fragmented. And it was successful in making the *New Journal* an amusing, interesting and readable piece of journalism, instead of the deadly boredom readers of older music publications had come to expect.

The personalities also appeared in Schumann's early music, most clearly in the *Davidsbündlertänze*, in which different movements were signed either by Florestan or Eusebius, or both, depending on the mood of the piece.

Davidsbündlertänze was one of the works that announced Schumann's genius to the world. Within its loose-knit framework, he created a world of wild imagination, humor and rich harmony. *Davidsbündlertänze,* composed in 1837, was a series of 18 different dances, each with an underlying emotional or literary message. Gaiety and high spirits alternate with quiet dreams of love, all ending at the midnight hour of a wedding night. The form of the piece stunned critics, who largely ignored it because they had no frame of reference for such a radical new concept; but the music was unquestionably splendid.

Schumann, the reviewer, wrote and edited with great creative integrity—never judging other composers in comparison to his own work. He strove to maintain complete independence, keeping his mind open to progress and never becoming a Philistine himself. Writing about Mendelssohn, Chopin and later, the young Johannes Brahms, his enthusiasm and admiration was clear.

The magazine served another important role in his life. Its development, along with a small publishing business, were part of his efforts to develop financial independence. The economics of being a composer had changed since the 18th century. Classical musicians had been well-behaved tradesmen who performed on cue for their patrons and didn't speak unless spoken to. In exchange for their services, they were paid small, regular salaries. Now, the patronage system was largely gone. Few kings or noblemen could afford the luxury of maintaining private orchestras and court composers. Composers were expected to sell their product on an open market, and depend on popular support to pay the rent. The new romantic musicians had much more freedom, but they had to buy it at the risk of going hungry. In this new age, it might be possible to become financially independent from the profits of subscription concerts and music publishing, or to make a solid living as a performer. But a great deal depended on the individual's ability to take reasonable care of money once it came through the door. Robert knew he had to become more responsible in managing his own money.

The years of watching his father's well-run business were not wasted, and Schumann's management of the *New Journal* helped lead him to a new fiscal maturity. While he would never achieve great wealth, Schumann did manage to survive financially—ultimately with the help of a working wife.

In the same year Schumann began publishing the *New Journal,* another important person entered his life— the beautiful Ernestine von Fricken. Compared to Clara, Ernestine was a woman of the world. She had shining raven hair, an elaborate wardrobe provided by her father the Baron and a full figure that immediately caught men's attentions. At the age of 18, her father sent her to study piano with Herr Wieck. She moved into Schumann's old bedroom in the Wieck home.

As Ernestine unpacked her trunks in June of 1834, Clara sat with rapt attention and listened to descriptions of romances and flirtations with young men in her hometown of Asch. "No one in Leipzig," said Ernestine, "could possibly be as handsome as they are."

"Oh, just wait until you meet our Herr Schumann," Clara answered.

Robert was at the Wieck home nearly every day. He and Clara worked together on new musical ideas, studying, composing and sharing ideas. In August of 1833, Clara had published a new piano composition, *Romance*, dedicated to Robert. It included a captivating melody which he turned around and used as a theme for some variations of his own. All their life was about music. But Ernestine's arrival changed the arrangement considerably. They still took long walks, but now they were accompanied by Ernestine, and the 15-year-old Clara realized she was suddenly being treated like a silly child. Clara was growing up, but Robert hadn't really noticed. He was much more interested in Ernestine, the experienced older woman of 18. Their growing romance was hard to ignore. Even Herr Wieck noticed the attachment.

Clara felt left out, but she didn't have much time to brood over the change in her relationship with Robert. She soon left on a concert tour and would not see him again for five months. In her absence, the relationship with Ernestine grew even more passionate. Robert was impressed not only with her obvious physical charms but also with the exalted position of her father, the Baron. He overlooked the fact that she wasn't really very bright and didn't have a great deal of musical talent.

Robert and Ernestine became secretly engaged, and her lack of interest in studying music or anything else except Herr Schumann became very apparent to Wieck. He immediately informed her father, the Baron, who appeared almost immediately in Leipzig and took her unceremoniously home. Clara was relieved, but she was still jealous.

Robert had gone to see Ernestine in Asch, causing him to miss one of Clara's concert performances. Clara's feelings were hurt, but she was patient, going to Dresden to study composition and leaving a lonely, love-sick Robert behind. His long-distance romance with Ernestine started to cool. Away from her physical charms, he began to notice that her letters were poorly written and badly spelled. And the last straw was the revelation that she was not a Baroness at all but the adopted, illegitimate daughter of the Baron. By the Spring of 1835, the romance was over, although Robert hadn't gotten around to telling Ernestine yet.

The most positive result of all this romantic frustration was Schumann's composition of *Carnaval* and another new piece, the *Études Symphoniques*, both more or less inspired by Ernestine. *Études Symphoniques* was based on a musical theme written by Ernestine's adopted father, the Baron von Fricken, a fine flute player and amateur composer. The musical portraits in *Carnaval* were all composed around the letters ASCH, Ernestine's home town and also the only musical letters in Robert's last name. Translated into notes (E-flat is Es in German, H is B natural) they form a recurring melody hidden throughout the composition. It was the same musical/literary trick he used in another composition, the *ABEGG* Variations. The literary device might have been a silly gimmick in the hands of a lesser artist, but in these pieces it didn't get in the way. Schumann the composer was beginning to hit full stride.

The *March of the Davidsbündler against the Philistines* in the *Davidsbündlertänze* was his battle cry for musical innovation, and it became the theme song for the writers who contributed to the *New Journal.* Business for the newspaper was good, with the subscription list growing larger each week. Robert Schumann was on his way to becoming a practical business executive. A growing maturity became evident to those who knew him, and his responsible management of the *New Journal* was a pleasant surprise even to Wieck, who had predicted it would fold in a month. Schumann began to take care of his money, pay his own bills and cut down on his consumption of Bavarian beer. The only vice he admitted he could not, or would not, discard was the smoking of good cigars. It was a habit he carried with him throughout his life.

Clara had grown too. When they were reunited in April of 1835, she was nearly 16. Walking into the Wieck parlor on a spring morning, Robert was astonished and completely tongue-tied. Sitting at the piano was a grown woman who barely resembled the thin little girl he had said goodbye to five months before. Her eyes, always her most remarkable feature, were now perfectly set in a lovely, oval face. Her figure was unmistakably changed. He was awestruck by the beautiful young woman who had come home. Throughout the summer, they were inseparable companions.

Schumann's compositions were becoming more sophisticated and more original. His Sonata in F-sharp minor, "Dedicated to Clara by Florestan and Eusebius," received its first public performance in the Wieck parlor, when Clara played it for Leipzig's newest musical star, Felix Mendelssohn.

Mendelssohn had just been appointed music director for the Gewandhaus, which was a great honor for someone only 26 years old. But it was a responsibility he was easily able to assume, for he had always done things at a young age. The child of a wealthy Jewish family in Berlin, Mendelssohn was a rare example of the happy, well-adjusted child prodigy. Performing and composing in his earliest years, by age 17 he had composed one of the world's most beloved overtures, *A Midsummer Night's Dream*.

Felix and Clara had become friends during her Paris stay, and her home was his first social call in Leipzig. She immediately introduced him to Schumann, and beginning a tradition of loyalty and good public relations, insisted on playing the new sonata. Mendelssohn was fascinated by the young composer's work, and Schumann in turn idolized Mendelssohn. The three continued their personal and musical collaboration throughout their lives.

Clara celebrated her sixteenth birthday with Schumann, Mendelssohn and other members of the Davidsbündler, who showered her with gifts, flowers and music. A few days later, another honorary member of the close musical society came to call. Chopin, in town for a visit, demanded that Mendelssohn take him to the Wieck's famous musical parlor. While Schumann sat shyly in the corner, tugging on his earlobe with embarrassment, Clara played all Schumann's compositions for Chopin, and then proceeded to play Chopin for Chopin. He admitted, "She plays them much better than I can play them myself." Mendelssohn wrote to his sister Fanny in awe, "She plays like a demon—or a witch."

Her skills polished to a fine edge, Clara was ready to take off on another extensive concert tour. Soon she and Robert would be separated for many months. The young couple was growing more and more attracted to each other, but although they were both skilled at expressing themselves musically they were very timid about discussing their new-found emotions.

The night before she left for her tour, Robert came to visit her. They sat for hours in the parlor, talking very little and then only about the music she would play at upcoming concerts. Finally, he knew he had to go. It was getting very dark. She carried a light down the stairs to show him the way out. Suddenly, he took her in his arms and kissed her. She almost dropped the light. "When you gave me your first kiss," she remembered, "I was very close to fainting. Everything became black before my eyes. I could scarcely hold the light which was to show you the way."

THE STRUGGLE FOR FULFILLMENT

*...a girl to whom I am completely bound by art,
mental affinity, habit of many years' friendship and
deepest, really holy love...*

—Robert Schumann

The first stop on Clara's concert tour was Zwickau. Robert said goodbye to her on the night of their first kiss and immediately went home to pack his bag. He would follow her at least that far on her travels. Backstage on the night of her performance, he surprised her with a bouquet of flowers and another kiss. As discreet as they might have been, there was no mistaking the happy flush of excitement on her face. Wieck observed the unavoidable truth—his daughter was in love with Robert Schumann.

He was astonished. In the first place, he was still under the assumption that Schumann was engaged to Ernestine. More than that, Schumann had been around the house since Clara was a little girl. Didn't he think of her as a little sister? But most deeply, he was stunned that *any* man would have the audacity to try and take Clara away from him. She was his life's work—the product of all his efforts. Everything she had become was the result of his genius. No one would snatch her away from him just at the moment he was ready to cash in on his investment.

Wieck flew into a rage. Clara was forbidden to see Schumann or to write to him. She would simply forget about him and all this absolute nonsense. "You are a great artist. Can you imagine yourself pushing a baby carriage? Idiocy!" She politely agreed with him and continued to exchange secret letters with Robert through an elaborate series of post office box drops and conspiratorial friends. When the concert tour was over, Wieck sent her back to Dresden for more composition lessons, certain he had put an end to the childish crush. He did not realize the stubbornness and patience of the young lovers.

The next month, in February of 1836, Robert's mother died. It was a crushing blow for a young man who was deeply, almost neurotically, devoted to his mother. The only thing greater than his grief was his fear of death. Terrified of going to her funeral, Robert instead went straight to the one person who could give him any comfort—Clara. He caught the first coach to Dresden and spent the next three days with her. Their love and their plans for a future together were the only thing that gave him any hope for the future. Finally, he was ready to make the funeral journey to Zwickau. Clara saw him off at the coach station, wearing a jaunty little red hat that did nothing to cheer up their gloom. They faced a long separation. After a tearful goodbye, Robert sat in the waiting room and wrote her a letter talking about their future together.

> *...you will be glad to continue as an artist, to work with me, share my burden, my joys and my sorrows. The waiting-room is growing dark. Passengers around me are asleep. Outside, gusts of wind and snow. But I shall bury myself deep in a corner with my head on a cushion and think of nothing but you. Farewell, my Clara.*

Clara did not attempt to keep the visit a secret. She was sure that her father would relent once he knew that their affection was not a passing whim. Instead, Wieck became violent and abusive. He threatened to kill Schumann on sight if he ever approached her or spoke to her again.

Wieck's rejection was very difficult for Schumann to understand. For years, he had loved and respected the older man, thinking of him almost as a father. He had even imagined that Wieck was training and educating him so he could be worthy to marry Clara. But despite Schumann's best efforts for the next three years, he would never win the father's consent. Ultimately, it became clear that Wieck didn't really object to Schumann at all, he would have resisted any man who took Clara away from his control. Wieck was passionately attached to his daughter and found it horrifying to think of any man taking his place in her affections.

His mother's death marked a turning point in Schumann's life. New-found financial skills were now essential to manage the small inheritance from his father's estate. His responsibilities had grown, and he appeared able to grow with them. The wild-eyed dreamer was gone. In his place was a sober, serious young man with two missions in life—to fulfill his musical genius and to marry Clara Wieck.

Clara and Robert had been close friends for many years, and he knew her character well. This new romance would prove to be one of the best urges Schumann ever gave in to. As a man who would increasingly need to be protected and insulated from the outside world, he could have made no better choice. Clara was a strong, independent woman, capable of holding off the whole world—she'd been doing that her whole life. Her skills would be put to the test severely during the years of their courtship and marriage. Fortunately for Schumann, she loved him passionately, and was willing to take on the responsibility of defending his genius. She was familiar with his moods and considered them a sign of his genius, not an emotional disease. Their growing affection was a source of stability at a time when his mental condition was often unstable.

As a child, Robert had been enthusiastic and outgoing. At 14, his personality began to change. He went through periods where he became unexplainably introverted, silent and passive. After his father's death, Schumann's mood swings became more dramatic and his periods of depression deeper.

Depression was common in the Schumann family, with both parents suffering from forms of the disease.

His father's "nervous condition" was probably chronic clinical depression. And while the argument still rages whether this illness is genetic or environmental, it does tend to happen frequently in certain families, for whatever reason. His mother's mood disorders were well documented and many of the same emotional problems were evident in Schumann's brothers and sisters, especially his sister Emilie, whose suicide at age 19 was a direct result of depression.

Regardless of whether it was inherited or the result of childhood trauma, Schumann had begun to show signs of emotional imbalance in adolescence. Of course, what we describe as "emotional imbalance," the 19th century called an "artistic temperament." There is no proof of a connection between this kind of emotional instability and creativity, but people of great talent often suffer from deep depressions. (Of course it could be argued that dull people of little talent can also become depressed, but we simply don't hear about it.) In practice, however, some of history's most creative people have been spurred on to productivity by trying to escape from the depths of depression. Frantic periods of work can fight off depression, and the result may be great art, or great thought.

Martin Luther, Abraham Lincoln and Winston Churchill all battled what Churchill called the "black dog" of depression. Schumann fought that same black dog all his life.

Schumann turned to music and literature as a means of fighting his illness. Although he was incapable of working during the deepest periods of depression, intense work could often hold back the onset of a bad episode. It was the same technique his father had used, and Schumann relied on it throughout his life. As a result, his most difficult periods were often his most productive.

Schumann found many ways to deal with an illness that often left him isolated and inarticulate. As the disease progressed, speaking became more of a labor. But he could still communicate through his music and his writing. When he fell in love with Clara, he might not be able to blurt out his feelings, but he could compose a passionate piano work. And when he couldn't express himself out loud to fellow-musicians, he could still write a charming and funny article that made his opinions very clear. As a result, his life was filled with friends and admirers, many of whom he scarcely spoke to in later years, but who remained dear to him.

The love he shared with Clara was one of few spoken words. But they shared their feelings in other ways, exchanging a flood of letters during their long courtship and sharing a common diary during their marriage—for writing down what couldn't be expressed out loud. It was a remarkable device for overcoming a handicap.

Having once made up his mind to wed Clara, Robert set out on a program of self-improvement. Realizing he wasn't the ideal suitor for such a remarkable young woman, he worked hard to overcome his financial limitations and weakness for champagne. Their extended courtship, for all its frustrations, allowed Schumann a chance to grow up.

When Clara was finally allowed to return to Leipzig, Wieck continued to forbid her to see or communicate with Schumann. Still completely controlled by her father, both financially and emotionally, she believed it was hopeless to fight his will. When he demanded it, she surrendered all Robert's letters and swore not to see him. Living in the same city, they did not exchange a word or a look for 16 months. Both of them tried to put the romance behind them and made tentative, hopeless attempts at other relationships.

In this darkest period, they both again turned to their music for consolation.

Robert composed his remarkable *Fantasie* in C major. Unable to express his feelings for Clara directly, he poured all his love into the *Fantasie*. The result is an explosion of emotion, melody and powerful musical expression—perhaps the most passionate music ever written for the piano. The *Fantasie's* three movements reach to the heights of happiness, fall to the depths of despair and ultimately climax in a triumphal finale that Schumann hoped would be reflected in his own real-life success in winning Clara's love.

Clara stormed the stage in a triumphal series of concert appearances, burying her sadness under relentless work. She was a phenomenal success in Berlin, astonishing her audiences by being the first person ever to play entire programs from memory, without the use of printed music. Wieck broke with another tradition by insisting that she appear alone with no other musicians, singers, orchestras or theatrical acts. Liszt was the only other pianist able to demand the spotlight in this way. Clara also presented a ground-breaking performance of Beethoven's *Appassionata* Sonata in Berlin. Always before, this complex and difficult piece had been considered unplayable and beyond audience understanding. Now she was acknowledged as its foremost interpreter.

The visit to Berlin was equally important because it brought about Clara's reunion with her real mother, now Frau Adolf Bargiel. They struck up an immediate friendship. A warmly sympathetic and understanding woman, Frau Bargiel was able to help her during this difficult time. Throughout the next three years, when Clara became increasingly alienated from her father, she turned to her mother for comfort and advice. They remained close friends throughout their lives.

Success followed success across Germany, until she returned to Leipzig in the summer of 1837. Clara was scheduled to play a concert there on August 13, but she had no hope of seeing Robert.

Enter Ernst Becker, fairy god-father.

Becker was a lawyer and music lover from Leipzig who liked both Clara and Robert. He also knew them well enough to realize they were miserable. Each was doing tremendous things professionally, but both were deeply lonely and still very much in love. Becker convinced Clara to include three of Schumann's *Symphonic Etudes* in her upcoming Leipzig concert. Her father would agree because he respected Schumann's work, even if he wouldn't accept him as a son-in-law. Becker promised to make sure Schumann was in the audience.

Clara and Robert were hesitant. Each was convinced the other had forgotten about their vows of eternal love. Neither had. Clara passed on a message through Becker. "Tell Robert to come and hear me play his *Etudes*. It is the only way I can show him that I still love him. I can speak to him only through his own music." Schumann and Becker sat in the back of the auditorium. She played with a fire and passion neither of them had ever heard. Schumann went home in a daze. She still loved him.

He quickly wrote her a letter filled with love and devotion. Becker secretly slipped the letter and a bouquet to Clara.

Becker's scheme had worked, the two lovers were back in contact and more determined than ever to be married. They carried on a secret correspondence, using her loyal maid, Nanny, as a go-between and even managed one secret meeting under an oak tree, with Nanny again standing guard. On Clara's eighteenth birthday, Schumann would send a letter to Wieck, asking for her hand.

A messenger delivered Schumann's letter. It was a careful, reasonable document, outlining his financial resources, career prospects and deep dedication to Clara's musical career. "If you find me to be a worthy and honest man, then bless this union of souls, whose complete happiness depends only upon your parental consent." Wieck met Schumann to discuss the letter.

"Thunderstorm," Clara called it. Cold hatred, deliberate hostility and demands for huge sums of money to reimburse Wieck for his "investment" in her career were Wieck's response. Clara was the goose about to lay the golden egg. Wieck wouldn't give her up without a fight. He began a series of venomous, vicious and violent attacks on Schumann. Schumann was absolutely crushed. Clara was emotionally ravaged. She still felt tremendous devotion and obligation to her father, who had been brainwashing her effectively for 18 years. But her love for Robert was equally profound. There were rough times ahead.

They had one more passionate meeting under the oak tree, with Nanny standing guard. Tears and kisses and more tears. It was to be their last touch for many months. Clara was going back on the road to Dresden, Prague and then Vienna. It would be seven months of smuggled letters carried by Nanny, letters written while standing up at the bureau with ink and paper hidden inside the drawer. Her father frequently walked in unannounced to check on her and was furious if she locked the door.

Remarkably, considering the emotional stress she was under, Clara was a financial and artistic success in Vienna. She achieved a celebrity status equal to that of Franz Liszt. Still she wrote to Robert almost every day. Her letters were filled with charmingly modest accounts of world-shaking events. "I have just played for the Empress and now I am eating a plate of soup."

The more successful she became, the more valuable a commodity she was to her father and the more determined he was not to share her with anyone. He continually whispered insults about Robert in her ear. She was still overawed by her father's influence, but as her self-confidence grew she was able to promise Robert she would never be frightened of her father again. Both of them were gaining insight into their own lives.

Robert wrote:

> *Perhaps I have been spoiled by having things made too easy for me, so it comes as all the more of a shock to be repulsed, insulted and slandered. I used to read about such things in novels, but I never expected to become the hero of such a fantastic family drama.*

Clara stayed in Vienna until April, again introducing Beethoven's *Appassionata* and prompting impassioned poetry in the local newspaper. The Emperor named her *Chamber Virtuosa to the Emperor*, an honorary title already conferred on Paganini, which put her in impressive company.

Once again, Franz Liszt was in town, giving breathtaking concerts and breaking the strings of every piano he played. He and Clara became good friends. Knowing his charm with the ladies, she could hardly have resisted him. He won her heart and she responded by playing him Schumann's music. Liszt was impressed with her playing and with Schumann's compositions. He wrote a powerful review of the newly published *Concerto for Piano without Orchestra*.

As successfully as Clara's career was progressing, her correspondence with Schumann never faltered. Through hundreds of letters, they discussed their future, negotiated how they would balance careers and family life, discussed where to live, had spats, made up and grew up. They decided to be married in 1840, when she would be of age.

Wieck now tried another tack. He and Clara had been planning a major tour to France. He now announced, "If Clara wants to go to Paris, she will have to go alone." He would not travel with her, handle bookings or make concert arrangements. "Let her have a taste of how painful the life of an artist can be," he said. "She'll come running back to me." Clara went to Paris on her own and proved him wrong, successfully wrestling with all the problems that faced a struggling artist.

Wieck tried yet another ploy. He gave Clara the impression that he would accept their marriage if they lived in Vienna. She passed the word on to Robert and he set off to Vienna, hoping that moving the magazine headquarters to a larger city would result in a larger income and a wider reputation. It didn't work. The Viennese music scene was far too stilted and the Austrian government censors were too rigid. But it didn't matter, because Wieck never had any intention of giving his permission anyway. There were, however, two great acquisitions on the trip. The first was a steel pen Robert found on Beethoven's grave. He superstitiously kept it and later used it to write his own great *Spring* Symphony.

The second and even more valuable discovery was an unknown symphony of Franz Schubert's, which Schumann found in an abandoned stack of manuscripts.

In the years between 1812 and 1817, Schubert had produced six complete symphonies. The seventh he only sketched but never orchestrated. In 1822, he began another, completing two movements, sketching a third and then putting the whole project into a drawer, where it was discovered after he died. Known as the *Unfinished Symphony,* it was a masterpiece, completely different in musical style from any symphony that had come before, and was immediately recognized as a breakthrough in symphonic development. It was called *Unfinished* because it contained only two movements, instead of the four that would have been traditional. But in every other way it was fully developed and complete. The music was dramatic and passionate, yet always under control. After finding the *Unfinished* Symphony, musical scholars of the time were still hoping to find more hidden works by Schubert. But when Schumann went to Vienna, not even Schubert's brother Ferdinand knew the late composer had left behind another masterpiece, the Symphony in C Major. When Schumann shuffled through the dusty piles of manuscript paper stored in Ferdinand's attic, he was ecstatic to find the massive work. It came to be called the *Great C Major,* partly because of its huge size, and also to distinguish it from Schubert's first C Major Symphony. Also called the *Symphony of Heavenly Length,* it is a powerful expression of Schubert's genius that soars and almost explodes with energy and power.

Schumann negotiated the publishing rights with Schubert's family and brought the manuscript back to Leipzig.

Wieck's abuse and manipulation of Clara had reached fever pitch. He began a public campaign to spread rumors and gossip about her. Deciding to destroy her career if he couldn't control it, he confiscated all her earnings from her previous concerts, which he could do under German law. She stayed in Paris.

Schumann finally made a dramatic decision and sent Clara a preliminary draft of a legal brief asking the High Court of Leipzig to grant them permission to marry without her father's consent. Her mother had already given her permission. Clara agreed and the documents were filed. Wieck was now completely out of control. He circulated poison pen letters about Schumann under fictitious names, refused to give Clara her winter coat, and wrote to piano manufacturers in Paris telling them not to let her use their pianos because she would break the strings.

The court asked the three of them to meet for arbitration, hoping to settle differences out of court. Clara returned from Paris and she and Robert sat in embarrassment at the Leipzig courthouse. Wieck never showed up. At the second hearing, he flew into a screaming rage—the judge threatened to throw him out of the courtroom. His campaign of lies and insults continued, to the point where Schumann filed suit against him for slander.

At their final meeting in Court, Wieck again became hysterical. His accusations against Schumann included: illegible handwriting, "too soft" voice, lazy disposition, inadequate income, lack of ability as a composer and author, infidelity, instability of character and being a drunkard. The court dismissed them all except the drinking allegation which Schumann returned to court and fought with character witnesses testifying to his sobriety. All of Wieck's charges were dismissed.

Now all that remained was to wait for the court's final decision. The outcome was certain, but the wheels of Saxon law ground slowly. Away from the disturbing influence of Wieck, the two enjoyed months of calm and happiness. Clara continued her concerts, living with her mother in Berlin when she wasn't on the road. Robert applied for and was granted an honorary degree of Doctor of Philosophy from the University of Jena. Mendelssohn began rehearsal of Schubert's *Great* C-major Symphony, which Schumann had rescued from oblivion in Vienna.

Liszt arrived and became good friends with Schumann—at least for the time being. Liszt had published an excellent review of Schumann's compositions and enjoyed praising him to anyone who would listen. Clara returned to Leipzig from a series of money-making concerts in Berlin and enjoyed sharing musical afternoons with Schumann and Liszt. "Liszt is something of a philanderer," she laughed, "but one soon forgets all that."

The couple traveled together to Berlin for Christmas with her mother and to play music with Mendelssohn, who was visiting his parents there. Still waiting for the court's decision, they returned to Leipzig and went house hunting, finding a quiet house on Inselstrasse, beyond the Old City, far from the noise of Leipzig's business district.

In July of 1840, the court gave Wieck one more opportunity to submit proofs of his charges or accept a decision against him. Finally, on August 12 the court officially sanctioned the marriage. Wieck was ordered to return at least part of Clara's earnings, her piano and her clothes. Nearly a year later, the court also found Wieck guilty of slander against Schumann and sentenced him to a short jail term.

On September 12, 1840, one day before Clara's twenty-first birthday, Robert Schumann and Clara Wieck were married. She wrote in her diary:

It was a beautiful day, and even the sun,
which had long remained hidden, suddenly

poured its mild rays upon us as we drove to the wedding, seeming to give its blessing to our union. Nothing disturbed us on this day and it shall be written down in this book as the happiest and the most important of my entire life...If I have known much trouble in my youth, I have also known much joy. I shall never forget that. Now a new life is beginning, a beautiful life, a life with the one whom I love above all...But serious duties are also facing me. May Heaven give me strength to fulfill them faithfully, like a good wife.

JOY AND MADNESS

*Well, so must it be when artists marry; one cannot
have everything; and after all, the chief thing is the
happiness which remains over and above, and we
are happy indeed in that we possess one another and
understand one another, understand and love with
all our hearts.*

—Robert Schumann

JOY AND MADNESS

The little house on Inselstrasse had a sunny garden and enough room for two grand pianos. Into her new home, Clara carried with her one of the most magnificent wedding gifts a bride ever received, a cycle of songs for voice and piano called *The Myrthen*. Robert gave her the specially bound volume of songs with a bouquet of myrthen, the Saxon equivalent of orange blossoms, on the night before their marriage. They were only part of a great outpouring of creative energy that celebrated Clara and Robert's marriage. In the three previous months, Robert had written almost 140 songs, including the *Liederkreis, Myrthen* and *Frauenliebe und-leben* song cycles. For a composer who had never before written for voice, it was a remarkable feat, and the songs have taken their place in music history as some of the most beautiful ever created.

German *lieder* (songs) were usually about sadness and the loss of love. Schubert mastered this tragic tradition in his song cycles. In *Die Winterreise (The Winter Journey)*, a man sick at heart because he has been betrayed by a woman travels through the winter countryside, identifying with the cold, lifeless nature that surround him. The music is tragic and painfully beautiful.

Schumann's lieder continue the traditional mode, based on poetry that recalls broken hearts, death and shattered romance. But listening to the music, it's difficult to hear much tragedy. Joy in his upcoming marriage shines in every phrase, and the melodies reflect happiness, contentment and fulfillment. He called 1840 "my song year."

After their frustrating five-year battle to be together, married life was a happy relief. Writing together in a shared marriage diary, they recorded a level of creative and personal compatibility that is surprising in two people of great creative gifts.

Robert opened up a wider world of literature and music to Clara, whose education had previously been limited by her father's single-minded goals. Together they composed another song cycle, studied Shakespeare and Goethe and Bach fugues. Robert composed almost constantly. Clara found it more difficult to make time for her work.

This was a serious conflict they struggled to solve. Clara's music suffered from a lack of a place to practice in their small apartment. She had her own piano, but the walls were paper thin and Robert could not bear hearing other music while he composed, so she remained silent. Eventually they reached a compromise. Each afternoon after he finished composing, Robert went down to the local cafe, read the paper and drank a beer. His absence gave Clara two hours for uninterrupted practice. It was still not enough, but it was the best they could manage. And now Clara had other important things on her mind; she was pregnant.

One year after the day of their marriage, Marie was born. The delivery was easy and both Schumanns welcomed her arrival. For the christening of their first child, Robert presented Clara with the first published copy of his new *Spring* Symphony, the manuscript of his newly completed D Minor Symphony and a first edition of *Twelve Songs*, a group of lieder they had composed together during her pregnancy. To a woman who valued the creation of music as life's ultimate pleasure, the manuscripts rivaled her daughter's birth in importance.

1841 was to be Schumann's symphony year. The *Spring* Symphony was performed under Mendelssohn's direction at Gewandhause concert on March 31. The presentation of this major work was an important breakthrough for Schumann, who did not want to limit himself to "small" piano compositions. If a composer was to be taken seriously, the production of symphonies was essential. Mendelssohn had written 17, and Schumann was determined to make his mark as well. The *Spring* Symphony featured Schumann at the height of his physical, mental and emotional powers. It is fresh and exciting music, more serious than his piano music, but still filled with lively humor and syncopation. Three more symphonies followed, each richer and more complex than the one before.

When Schumann composed, he became totally and absolutely absorbed in his work, completely forgetting about other people. Sometimes Clara complained that he was cold and ignored her, but she knew this was the price she had to pay for the magnificent work he was doing. When the work was finished and he came out of his trance, he again became a warm, affectionate husband and father, apologizing for his distance. But as soon as the creative urge came upon him again, he went back in his shell. It was a pattern she came to recognize and accept.

From this point on in his life, Schumann increasingly withdrew from human contact for long periods of time. Always subject to depression alternating with frantic work, his periods of withdrawal grew more frequent and more prolonged. Ferdinand David, concertmaster of the Gewandhaus, wrote this description of a meeting with the distracted composer:

> *Schumann came to me yesterday, and remained without speaking for a whole hour. From this I gathered that he would not be averse to hearing his symphony once more in public. I hinted that it would be better for him to hear the horns rehearse; on which he made it clear by signs that he would willingly pay for a rehearsal to make the work go thoroughly well. After he smoked two cigars, he rubbed his mouth twice, as if to prevent a single syllable from coming out, took his hat, forgot his glove, nodded his head, tried the wrong door, and at last got away through the right one.*

Within two month's of Marie's birth, Clara was again ready to begin performing, joining Robert for a presentation of his symphony in the city of Wiemar. Her own compositions were receiving excellent reviews, especially the *Trio for Piano, Violin and Cello,* her most ambitious work. Working in a more structured, classical form than Schumann, she still managed to fill the music with tenderness and romantic lyricism. One violinist who admired her work was the young prodigy Joseph Joachim, who was studying composition with Mendelssohn. He said, "Mendelssohn had a big laugh because I would not believe that a woman could have composed something so sound and serious."

But composition was difficult to fit into her busy life. In their diary, Schumann observed:

> *Clara has written a number of small pieces that show a musical and tender invention*

that she has never attained before. But to have
children and a husband who is always living in
the realms of imagination do not go together
with composing. She cannot work at it regularly
and I am often disturbed to think how many
profound ideas are lost because she cannot work
them out.

Clara was anxious to begin touring again. Concert
performers had to stay constantly in the public eye or risk
losing their audience. What's more, the impoverished
young couple desperately needed the revenue. But
Robert wanted to stay home. The stress of travel made him
depressed and sick, and took him away from composition
and management of the *New Journal*. What's more, he
found it very difficult to tag along in the role of Clara
Schumann's husband. Although his music was becoming
increasingly well-known, she was the center of attention,
and he resented being ignored. Clara tried going on tour
alone, but despite her success in Copenhagen, the six-
week separation from Robert and her daughter were hard
on all of them. This conflict continued throughout their
marriage and was never resolved successfully.

Schumann's health deteriorated and the change in
his physical condition was reflected in his face. Gone was
the beautiful youth. Now his face was heavy and immo-
bile, his mouth constantly pinched into a facial contortion
that made him look like he was whistling a silent tune. He
often remained silent for hours, and speech became
increasingly difficult. But his ability to express himself in
music never decreased.

It is difficult to imagine how a man in such a state of
mental turmoil could compose works that are so serene
and clear-headed. He completed three string quartets, a
piano quartet and the masterful piano quintet, all destined

to become classics. In contrast to his personal withdrawal, these chamber music works are outgoing, energetic and confident.

Schumann tried his hand at teaching in Mendelssohn's new Leipzig Conservatory of Music, but his inability to speak in public made him a very poor teacher. Clara, who would have been a more successful teacher, could not join the staff of the Conservatory because she was expecting another child.

After the birth of their second daughter, Elise, Robert joined Clara on an exhausting tour of Russia that lasted five months. When they returned to Leipzig, Robert suffered a complete mental and physical breakdown. He trembled constantly and suffered from a terrible fear of heights and sharp metal objects. Worst of all, he heard constant noises and aural delusions that made composing impossible. He gave up editorship of the *New Journal* and his teaching job at the Conservatory. The couple moved to Dresden, hoping that a change of scenery would improve his health.

The change of scenery did help and the Dresden years were productive. His health improved and his reputation as a composer grew.

The Schumann family grew too. Four more children were born to Clara between the years of 1845 and 1849. She had greeted the birth of their first two children with joy. But, she became more and more depressed with each new pregnancy. When she discovered she was pregnant for a fifth time, Clara wrote in her diary:

> *What will become of my work? Yet Robert says "children are blessings" and he is right...so I have decided to face the difficult time that is coming as cheerfully as possible. Whether it will always be like this, I don't know.*

Clara's career remained stable, but she limited her concerts to local areas in order to care for Robert and her children. During these years, Robert's greatest joy was his family. Within the protected environment of his home, he was cheerful and outgoing in a way that outsiders never saw. The happiness he felt is reflected in his famous *Album for the Young,* composed in 1848. It is a collection of 44 miniatures specially composed for children.

> *I wrote the first pieces as a birthday offering to my eldest daughter and added the others at subsequent intervals. It seemed to me as if I were once more just beginning to compose, and you will even find traces of my old humor appearing every now and then.*

The greatest musical triumph of this period was the Piano Concerto in A minor, among the best loved of all romantic works for piano and orchestra. It began as a single-movement *Fantasy for Piano and Orchestra* written for Clara, and eventually developed into a major virtuoso display. Reflecting his emotions of the moment, the concerto is moody, complex and spiritual. It remains a modern, innovative piece of work today, still drawing its power from Schumann's imagination.

In November of 1848, the Schumann's dear friend, Felix Mendelssohn, died suddenly from a stroke at the age of 39. Mendelssohn's death triggered even worse depression and Schumann's health began to go downhill. His condition was further aggravated by the political turmoil that hit Dresden in May of 1849. Following the example of the Paris insurrection, crowds rushed into the streets, threw up barricades and bitter hand-to-hand fighting spread throughout the city. Clara and Robert shared the rebel's democratic ideals, but neither had any stomach for the violence they saw around them. Corpses were stacked

on the sidewalk near their home and roving gangs went
door to door, forcing men into service on the barricades.

When the rebels knocked on her front door, Clara
sent them away, but she knew they would return. Taking
a disoriented Robert and her eldest daughter, she left her
younger children with a maid and fled across the field to
the nearby village of Maxen. It was a six-hour journey on
foot but Clara, who was six months pregnant, made it
twice, returning for her other children under cover of
night. When the fighting subsided, suppressed by Prussian troops, they returned to Dresden. But by fall 1849,
they were anxious to leave the shattered city. When
Schumann was offered a permanent position as musical
director for the city of Düsseldorf, he decided to accept.

Düsseldorf was a beautiful and friendly city. The
Schumanns were received warmly, with the respect that
two such musical celebrities deserved. But the decision to
take a director's position was a disaster for the silent and
mentally distraught composer. His conducting had never
been his great strength and now he found himself almost
completely unable to manage the demanding schedule of
choral and orchestral performances. Clara became his
voice. Standing before the orchestra, Schumann would
look to Clara with a pleading, confused look on his face.
Sitting next to him at the piano, she would would tell the
orchestra, "The Maestro would like you to play that
passage more pianissimo, please." Stories of his embarrassing mental confusion became common jokes. He
often kept beating time to the music long after a piece had
ended, not seeming to notice that the music had stopped.
And he dropped the baton so often, Clara was forced to
tie it to his wrist with a piece of string.

The Schumann's relationship with the Orchestral
Committee and the city deteriorated. Schumann had
always been stubborn, and now he was growing paranoid

too, convinced that members of the orchestra and his assistant conductor were conspiring to replace him. In fact, the committee that had been so pleased to hire him was now at a loss as to what to do with him. Clara defended him in the face of all realistic facts. She seemed unable to accept his decline, even when he cruelly included her in his paranoid fantasies. His assistant conductor gradually took on more of the conducting duties, but the conductor and his employers were at an impasse. Schumann was losing his hold on sanity, however the appearance of a new friend brought him a joyful, six-month reprieve.

On a September morning in 1853, a young man appeared at the door of the Schumann residence at No. 23 Bergenstrasse. He was wearing a road-weary gray alpaca coat, carrying a knapsack filled with music manuscripts and clutching a letter of introduction from their friend, Joseph Joachim. He was a striking figure, shifting nervously from one foot to the other on the front steps—so remarkable an image that the Schumann's eldest daughter, Marie, would still remember him vividly 60 years later. He was tall, with a broad handsome face and a long mane of thick, blond hair covered with the dust of two months walking journey down the Rhine. Johannes Brahms had come to play his music for the Schumanns.

Brahms' appearance asking for an audience wasn't unusual. Dozens of aspiring musicians made the pilgrimage to Düsseldorf each year and were welcomed into the Schumann's cheerful family. He had arrived at the appointed hour today to play his music for the masters. A maid escorted him into the music room overflowing with two large grand pianos, thousands of books on great mahogany shelves, and walls filled with photographs, drawings and testimonials to the couple's international renown. It was the center of the Schumann home, and their lives were clearly reflected in its crowded domesticity.

The room was an absolute contrast to the imperial splendor of the great home in Weimar where the virtuoso Franz Liszt held court. Brahms had left there a week before, finding its grandness overwhelming to a boy from the slums of Hamburg. He had been so nervous and uncomfortable in Liszt's presence that he had been unable to play his compositions. Here, however, he immediately felt at home. In this room it would be easy to play his music.

Herr Schumann shuffled into the room. His now stout figure was wrapped in a rumpled purple bathrobe and he was wearing leather bedroom slippers. He smiled warmly at young Brahms and shook his hand, but said nothing understandable, only murmured an unintelligible greeting and motioned toward the piano. Schumann sat down in a leather chair, clasped his hands and whispered, "Play for me, please."

Brahms sat down at the grand piano and immediately began playing; his long, expressive fingers moving with grace and speed over the keys. He had played for only a few moments when Schumann abruptly stood up and motioned for him to stop. Brahms was stunned, but Schumann quickly walked over to his side, put both hands on his shoulders and said, "Wait a moment, Clara must hear this."

Schumann disappeared and came back with Clara on his arm. "Now my dear Clara," he said to her, "You shall hear such music as you have never heard before; and you, young man, play the work from the beginning."

Brahms played everything he had and then, at their request, played it all again. The music they heard was powerful and deeply moving. It was structured in a classical style, at first appearance more conservatively constructed than the whimsical first works of Schumann. But it was firmly rooted in the romantic tradition, obviously influenced as much by Schumann's own work as that of earlier composers. The three of them happily went through all his compositions, ate lunch and played them yet again. He ended up staying more than a month.

Johannes Brahms was the child of a poverty-stricken Hamburg musician and a crippled seamstress who married late in life. Their home in the slums of Hamburg was a decaying brick and timber tenement with laundry hanging out the windows and prostitutes leaning on its front porch. As a child, Johannes showed unusual musical talent. His parents had great hopes for him, struggling to pay for piano and composition lessons with Eduard Marxsen, the best teacher in Hamburg. Marxsen was so impressed with the boy's abilities that he soon stopped charging for the lessons. Brahms' childhood was clouded by sexual abuse at the hands of local prostitutes, but his passion for composing and performing never failed him. Music gave him solace as a child and provided him with an escape from the slums.

The Hungarian violinist, Eduard Remény, selected young Brahms to accompany him on a European concert tour, and the young man left his Hamburg home when he was twenty. The partnership was a failure, but it had one successful result. Remény introduced Brahms to one of his idols, the violinist Joseph Joachim. Joachim and Brahms began a friendship and professional association that was to last 50 years. At Joachim's urging, Brahms traveled to Düsseldorf to meet Robert and Clara Schumann.

The meeting of the three musicians was to have fateful consequences for them all. Schumann had found the successor who would carry his romantic musical ideas forward into the next century. Brahms was propelled by Schumann's support into the forefront of the musical world. And Clara met the man whose life and career would be deeply intertwined with her own for the rest of her life.

Schumann was astonished by the boy's power as a composer, and immediately began a campaign to make his music known to the public. He wrote to his own music publisher and insisted that they release all of Brahms' existing compositions. Then he sat down at his old writing desk and composed an article that was to make Brahms famous. The *New Journal* had long ago moved into other hands, but Schumann now wrote an essay titled "New Paths" that sang the praises of young Brahms.

It said, in part:

> *I felt certain that from such developments would suddenly emerge an individual fated to give expression to the times in the highest and most ideal manner, who would achieve mastery, not step by step, but at once, springing like Minerva fully armed from the head of Jove. And now here he is, a young fellow at whose cradle graces and heroes stood watch. His name is Johannes Brahms.*

It was high praise coming from the critic who had first recognized Chopin's great talent.

But Schumann's happy months with Brahms were only a last brief moment of light before darkness descended. On February 6 of 1854, he wrote his last, confused letter to Joseph Joachim.

> *I have often written to you in sympathetic ink; and also between the present lines there is a secret writing that will later emerge. And I have*

*dreamed of you, dear Joachim...Your hands
were full of heron-feathers, and out of them
flowed champagne...The music is silent now—
at least outwardly...Now I will end. Already it
grows dark.*

He began to hear music, sung by choirs of angels.
Then the angels changed to demons and screaming
hyenas and tigers that attacked him. Sometimes he could
write down the melodies the angels sang to him, but more
often he was paralyzed by horrifying fear and physical
pain.

Clara called in doctors who could do nothing to calm
him or end the aural and visual hallucinations. The
visions, and the mystical music, continued. In an afternoon of lucid thought, he sat down with Clara and told
her, " I must go to an asylum. Don't worry, it won't be for
long. I will be well soon." Then he went into the bedroom,
packed his clothes and wrote out his will. Yet the next day
he sank into a terrible depression.

Slipping past the guard who was supposed to be
watching him, he left the house in bathrobe and slippers,
ran to a bridge over the Rhine river and jumped in. Two
fisherman in a boat pulled him from the water and took
him home, where he again asked to be committed to an
asylum. This time his wish was granted. Clara, who was
pregnant with their eighth child, remembered this of his
departure:

*Oh, God! now the carriage stood at our
door. Robert, having dressed in great haste,
entered the carriage with Dr. Hasenclever and
two guards, without a word or inquiry about me
or the children. And I sat...in dazed stupefac-
tion and thought—now I must die!...I had slipped
Dr. Hasenclever a bouquet for him, and this was*

passed along during the drive. He held it long in his hand without noticing it; then he smelled it, smiled and pressed the doctor's hand. Later, he gave a flower to everyone in the carriage. The doctor brought me his. I kept it, but my heart bled!

She would not see him again for two years. Their next meeting was on the day before he died.

The decision to hospitalize Schumann filled Clara with a terrible mixture of sorrow and relief. As his personality had disintegrated, he had become very difficult to live with. The man who had once been so intelligent and thoughtful had become distracted and inaccessible. The husband who had always adored her had become harsh, critical and cold. Now he was gone and she could breathe a sigh of relief. But he wasn't really gone. His presence a few miles away in the hospital was like a living death. For the next two years she was held in limbo—unable to go on with her life or put aside her grief and guilt about her husband.

The only bright spot in this dark time was young Johannes Brahms. Immediately upon hearing about Schumann's collapse, he hurried back to Düsseldorf to help Clara. All her friends gathered around her at this time, but Brahms was the most devoted. He had no pressing job or family responsibilities, so he could completely dedicate himself to caring for the Schumann family. For the next three years he was Clara's almost constant companion.

Brahms moved into the Schumann apartment in Düsseldorf and immediately took over care of the children, keeping the books and running the family finances, while continuing work on new compositions. During this time, he began work on his first symphony, wrote a set of ballades and created a special set of variations for Clara based on one of Robert's old tunes.

Brahms was one of the few visitors the hospitalized Schumann ever asked for. For the first ten months of his stay, the doctors allowed no visitors. Trying to protect a pregnant and distraught Clara, they had advised her not to visit her husband. What's more, he rarely ever asked about her or the children, and did not want to see anyone from his family. The enforced separation made his hospitalization even more difficult for Clara.

One night in May, a friend from Leipzig visited Clara and made this record:

> *My longing to see Clara Schumann pre-vailed over my shyness toward this celebrated artist. We came to Schumann's kitchen first, from there went to the children's room, where the nurse asked us to wait because "the Frau Doktor" was playing just now but we could listen from outside. The playing sounded grand, serious and powerful; we could not understand how she could play like that at this time. When the piece was over (I didn't recognize it though it was familiar), she came out; she looked so pathetic that it was difficult not to embrace her immedi-ately. She was altered, looked old and jaun-diced, but not broken or tearful. We avoided talking about the misfortune; she asked after friends and why her father had not written for so long. Then she...struggled against tears and burst out in bitter sobs. "If I didn't have the firm hope that my husband would be better soon, I wouldn't want to live anymore. I cannot live without him. The worst is that I may not be with him and he has not yet asked for me, not even*

once during the whole time." She could barely bring out these words, they were interrupted by convulsive sobs and her lovely eyes looked at me in an unspeakably sorrowful way. "But don't think," she continued, "that my husband is so bad. You would hardly notice that he was ill, he can carry on the deepest conversation, and is totally clear about his situation; he went to the institution voluntarily so he could return to us all the sooner.

The music her friend heard was Brahms' C major sonata, played by the composer. That night, May 7, 1854, was his twenty-first birthday.

One month later, Clara gave birth to her eighth child, a boy named Felix after her late friend, Felix Mendelssohn.

When Schumann was finally allowed visitors, he asked for Brahms and Brahms' music. Even at this early age, Brahms' compositions showed the promise that would one day make him a master of modern symphonic composition. Schumann took tremendous pleasure reading Brahm's new compositions as soon as they were completed. This relationship continued until Schumann slipped into complete incoherency. Clara also was deeply involved in Brahms' musical development, and was profoundly moved each time he played her his newest compositions. In this sense, too, he filled the same place in her life that Schumann had filled. For the next 40 years, the shared joy of music, its composition and performance would draw them together.

The private hospital where Schumann was staying was a pleasant, positive place. He lived in his own apartment with a piano and a garden. He and Brahms often played music together and walked for hours. After the first few months of his stay there, Brahms noticed a small improvement. The composer seemed more calm and more rational and his doctors thought there might be a chance of recovery.

In the meantime, he and Clara had to find ways to support the family and the cost of an expensive sanitarium. Fortunately, the city of Düsseldorf was gracious enough to continue his salary and that small but regular amount was invaluable over the first year. Brahms had no money of his own, so he began taking on piano students. Clara was anxious to avoid taking charity from friends. As soon as her son Felix was born, she began planning an extensive concert tour to raise capital. Always able to rely on work to pull her through periods of stress, Clara returned to her old habits, accepting every possible engagement. From 1854 until 1856, she relentlessly kept up a schedule of concerts in Berlin, Vienna, Prague, Budapest, Belgium, the Netherlands and England. For much of this time, Brahms stayed in Düsseldorf with the children. He had taken over the role of head of the household—in many ways. In addition to caring for the family, Brahms had become Clara's closest friend and strong supporter. They developed a powerful bond that was to make them companions and compatriots until their deaths. He struggled to cheer her up, encouraged her when she was tired and—she slowly came to realize—fell in love with her.

Whether or not their relationship was ever consummated has been a question of scholarly debate for the last 100 years. They took great pains to keep that information to themselves, though unquestionably there were rumors. Certainly there were opportunities. They were virtually inseparable for the two years of Schumann's hospitalization, and there is no doubt that they loved each other deeply. But most modern biographers believe that their mutual love and admiration for Schumann, combined with Clara's strict self-discipline, probably resulted in a platonic rather than sexual relationship. And if the truth be told, it's probably none of our business.

Hope for Schumann's recovery dwindled during his second year of hospitalization. The illness that was destroying him progressed rapidly now, causing him to lose the powers of speech, motor control and hearing.

What killed Robert Schumann? It was a confusing illness that suggested a wide variety of possible causes, ranging from schizophrenia to brain tumors. Modern scholars, in a medical detective story, have discussed the symptoms and medical evidence for years. The consensus is that Schumann suffered from two, unconnected illnesses. One a psychological disorder and the other an organic disease of the brain.

All the nervous symptoms which troubled Schumann in early life and up to the age of 42 were related to his chronic mood disorder, commonly called manic depression. The disease that ultimately killed him was much different.

Beginning in 1843, he complained of dizziness and then noticed noises in his ears that sounded like constant musical tones. Painful rheumatic aches of his joints and bones followed, along with deterioration of speech and coordination. The next year he suffered a minor stroke that further damaged his speech. Profound visual and auditory hallucinations finally drove him to attempt suicide. His intellectual deterioration continued until he became completely incoherent.

According to modern medical thinking, the only disease that could have resulted in these symptoms was syphilis of the central nervous system. Syphilis was rampant in 19th century Europe and virtually untreatable. Often it killed its victims within two or three years. But in some cases, the disease went into remission and lay dormant for many years before attacking the central nervous system and brain.

But syphilis is highly contagious. If Schumann had acquired it during his indiscreet younger days in Leipzig, why didn't he pass it on to his wife and children after his marriage? This has been a question that puzzled many researchers who found no record of Clara ever contracting the disease and no evidence of its being present in their children. The answer lies in the types of treatment that were available for syphilis at the time. Antibiotics were not available and no permanent cure was then known, but doctors had developed other limited treatments that made a patient non-infective. One of the most common was the use of mercury. In minute doses, it could prevent a patient from passing on the disease to his sexual partner. Unfortunately, it did not completely cure the disease and could result in fatal complications later.

One difficult side-effect of the mercury treatment was a form of muscular paralysis that can affect those treated with unnecessarily large doses. In fact, the mysterious 'injury' that struck Schumann's hand in the early 1830s may actually have been paralysis resulting from mercury treatment for syphilis. But it is impossible to prove or disprove any of these theories, and so the true cause of his final illness will always remain unknown.

In April of 1856, Clara went to England for a concert tour, where she played 26 concerts in less than three months. This pattern of endless travel and hectic concert schedules, which she had become used to as a child, was to continue throughout her life. To some extent, it was required by the financial demands of her large family. However, Clara knew that performing gave her great artistic satisfaction—and kept her mind off loneliness and grief. While many, including Brahms, were concerned that her rigorous schedule was a drain on Clara's strength, she seemed to thrive on it. As a result of her constant performing and touring, Clara Schumann became one of Europe's most renowned concert artists. She used her fame to promote the works of Robert Schumann and Johannes Brahms.

When she returned to the continent, she received a letter from the asylum saying, "If you want to see Robert alive, come at once." She and Brahms traveled there, only to discover the crisis had passed and the doctors would not let her see their patient. She left but returned again on the twenty-seventh of July 1856. She wrote:

> *Between six and seven that evening I saw him. He smiled at me, and with a great exertion—for he could no longer control his limbs—put his arm about me—I will never forget it. That embrace I would not trade for all treasures...It seemed that he kept talking much with spirits, could not long stand anybody about him, which made him uneasy; but one could no longer understand him. Only once did I catch "my." Surely he wished to say "Clara" for at the same time he gave me a friendly glance; then once more, "I know"—probably "you."*

At four o'clock the next day, while all his friends were out of the room, Robert died quietly in his sleep. He was only 46 years old.

Robert Schumann was buried in Bonn at the Old Cemetery, beneath five tall trees. The funeral was small, with only a few invited guests following the casket to its grave. Standing next to Clara was her dearest friend and Robert's greatest admirer, Johannes Brahms. That day marked a dramatic turning point in their lives. Brahms' greatest work lay ahead of him, but Clara would never compose again. From that day on, her music would only be the music of others.

TWO OLD FRIENDS

Doing one's duty is what brings happiness.

—Clara Schumann

Clara Schumann was a 36-year-old widow with seven children to support. After Robert's death her grief was very real, but she had little time to indulge in it. The need to begin work was pressing, but before she could start work, one more thing had to be resolved—her relationship with Brahms.

A month after Schumann's death, Clara, her sons Ludwig and Ferdinand, Brahms and his sister Elise all went on a walking trip through the Rhine Valley. The purpose of the trip was to help Clara regain her strength. It also gave Clara and Johannes time to discuss their futures. We don't know for sure what they decided, because all Clara's letters about the subject were later destroyed and her diary doesn't reveal anything. But we do know the ultimate result: once the journey was over, Clara and Brahms went their separate ways. Committed as they were to a lifetime of friendship, they would not marry.

After the vacation, eight-year-old Ludwig and seven-year-old Ferdinand were sent to boarding school in Bonn. The other children were scattered. Marie and Elise, who were 15 and 13 at the time of their father's illness, were at boarding school in Leipzig. Julie had been sent to Berlin to live with her grandmother. Only the two youngest children remained with Bertha. Brahms and Clara both left Düsseldorf in October. Brahms headed back to Hamburg and a new life of his own. Clara began a concert tour that was to continue virtually unbroken for the next 35 years.

The stories of her children reflect the sadness of her later life.

MARIE SCHUMANN 1841-1929

Marie enjoyed a close relationship with her mother, and after her father's death, took on much of the responsibility for raising the other children. She never married and remained with Clara throughout her life, acting as companion, traveling partner and seamstress. When Clara retired from the concert stage in 1878 and took a teaching position at the Frankfurt Conservatory, Marie joined her there as a teaching assistant and worked tirelessly to help Clara edit the complete editions of Robert Schumann's work. When Clara retired, so did Marie. Marie became the guardian of the Schumann family legend, taking possession of her mother's diaries after her death and supervising the writing of her father's biography. She retired to Interlaken, Switzerland after her mother's death and lived there the rest of her life.

ELISE SCHUMANN SOMMERHOFF 1843-1928

Elise declared her independence from the powerful influence of her mother and set off to make a life for herself. After studying piano with her mother and appearing with her in public, Elise decided that the pressure of performance—and her mother's criticism and demands—were too intense. She left home, working as a governess and lady's companion until she was 34, when she married

Louis Sommerhoff, a German business man with interests in America. They moved to America for six years and then returned to Germany, where she and her husband maintained a warm and supportive relationship with Clara in her final years. They had four children, three of whom lived to adulthood. Elise's descendents today live in Germany and the United States. None of them are professional musicians.

JULIE SCHUMANN, CONTESSA MARMORITO DI RADICATI 1845-1872

Julie was the prettiest and the most fragile of all the Schumann children. After her father's death she never lived with her mother, and was placed first with her grandmother and then with a series of wealthy, affectionate family friends who could keep her in sunny climates and near good doctors. She married a widowed Italian Count 1869. In bad health for most of her life, she became ill after the birth of her second child. She died of tuberculosis during her third pregnancy, at the age of 27. Descendents of her son, Roberto, still live in Turin, Italy.

EMIL SCHUMANN 1846-1847

Little Emil was very ill from his birth until his death at the age of 16 months. According to family records, he died of "glandular" disease.

LUDWIG SCHUMANN 1848-1899

Ludwig was a cheerful, affectionate little boy who began showing signs of "oddness" as an adolescent. He spent most of his young life away at school, first in a college preparatory program and then in a more menial trade school. By the time he was 22, Ludwig's behavior was so bizarre that Clara sent him to a psychiatric clinic for observation. The doctors' diagnosis was a spinal disease affecting his brain. He was judged incurably insane. Clara committed him to the insane asylum in Colditz, just south of Leipzig. It was the same institution that young Robert Schumann had visited when it was supervised by Dr. Carus—a forbidding castle whose memory had haunted Schumann throughout his life.

Clara kept in close touch with the hospital administrator, but she did not visit Ludwig until four years after his commitment. The horror of seeing him there left her in agony, stirring again the painful memory of Schumann's madness. She returned one year later, in response to Ludwig's letters begging her to have him released. Her visit left her convinced that Ludwig had to stay in the hospital, and as far as we know, she never saw him again. He remained in the hospital until his death in 1899.

FERDINAND SCHUMANN 1849-1891

Ferdinand's relationship with his mother was sadly reminiscent of her own dealings with Friedrich Wieck. Clara was stern, unforgiving and demanding of Ferdinand, and he was constantly reminded of his failure to live up to her expectations. Drafted into the Franco-Prussian War of 1870, he served with distinction, but fell victim to debilitating rheumatism. The disease was treated with morphine, to which he became addicted. When he ran up gambling debts and was unable to work in his profession of banking because of the ongoing addiction, Clara took over management of his wife and six children. She had never approved of Ferdinand's young wife, and now she was responsible not only for supporting her but for determining their children's living arrangements and education. Like her father, Clara constantly struggled to dominate and control her children's and grandchildren's behavior.

The responsibility and financial burden of the six grandchildren was serious, but Clara, grimly determined to handle her responsibilities, worked even harder to meet the challenge. Ferdinand's eldest daughter, Julie, was sent to private school in Berlin. Clara's eldest grandson, Ferdinand, lived in Frankfurt with his grandmother and aunts, while the younger boys were sent to live with another relative. Clara's son, Ferdinand, died from the effects of morphine addiction when he was 42. His widow, Antonie, hated Clara and blamed her for Ferdinand's death.

The family was split by bitter disputes, with Alexander, another of Ferdinand's sons, siding with his mother, Antonie. He later published a vicious "biography" of his grandmother that claimed Brahms was the father of her last child, Felix. Marie and Eugenie tried to buy all the copies and destroy them, but a few became public.

In the end, it was her grandson Ferdinand who was the only grandchild to remain close to Clara. He was with her, playing a piece by his grandfather, when she died.

EUGENIE SCHUMANN 1851-1938

The youngest of the Schumann daughters, Eugenie received an excellent education at boarding schools and exceptional musical training at a music academy in Berlin. The academy was directed by her mother's old friend, Joseph Joachim. A gifted musician, Eugenie lived at home until she was 40, at which time she set off on her own musical career. She taught and performed in England for 20 years, returning home to be with her mother when she died. After her mother's death, Eugenie shared with Marie the responsibility of protecting the Schumann family legend, writing two books about the family, *Erinnerungen (Memoirs)* and *Robert Schumann: Ein Lebensbild Meines Vaters (A Portrait Of My Father)*.

FELIX SCHUMANN 1854-1879

Born while his father was in the asylum, Felix inherited more of his father's talent than any of the other children. He was named after Felix Mendelssohn, tutored by Brahms and dreamed of becoming a poet and musician. Unfortunately, Felix began to show symptoms of tuberculosis in his adolescence and died of the disease at age 24. Brahms used three of Felix's poems for some of his loveliest—and most poignant—songs.

When Clara and Brahms separated after Schumann's death, Brahms returned to his home in Hamburg. He appeared at the Hamburg Philharmonic Concerts as soloist in Beethoven and Schumann piano concertos. He began to compose and teach and was soon invited to visit the court of Lippe-Detmold, a tiny principality whose ruler, Prince Leopold, had established a choral society and a small court orchestra. The young composer made a good impression with his playing, in spite of his rough language and poor manners. The Prince offered him a regular appointment in Detmold to direct the orchestra and chorus and give lessons to the Princess Frederike from October to December of each year. Brahms accepted the appointment, which would give him some financial security and still allow time for composition and touring. Clara sold her house in Düsseldorf and moved her family to Berlin. Being close to her mother gave her some comfort, and with Brahms gone, she needed more help with the children who remained at home.

For the next three years, Brahms spent three months in Detmold and the rest of his year touring, composing and spending time with Clara and her family during their vacations.

Brahms worked extensively on a large-scale piano concerto based on his earlier attempt at a symphony. It was the source of endless difficulty for him. Working with Joachim, he rehearsed it with the Hanover orchestra in a private session during 1848, but would not publicly perform it until 1859.

When in Hamburg, Brahms lived with his parents in a larger, more comfortable apartment he helped them pay for. He had a strong sense of loyalty to Hamburg and his parents and spent a lot of time there in hope of building his local reputation. He hoped to be appointed to some kind of permanent position, but found that musicians—as well as prophets—are often not respected in their own home towns.

In Detmold, conducting a chorus filled with stuffy noble ladies he called "his serene highnesses," was the only amusement Brahms could find. Life in Hamburg with his parents was equally lonely. But in the city of Göttingen, where he spent his summers, things were much more interesting. He stayed at the home of his friend Julius Otto Grimm, an excellent musician he had befriended in Leipzig. Grimm had recently been appointed musical director in Göttingen and married Phillipine Ritmüller, the daughter of a wealthy piano maker. Their home was filled with music and musicians living a gay, uninhibited lifestyle. Brahms was happy and relaxed in Göttingen, and his music was well received, especially by a dark-eyed, lively, intelligent girl with long black hair and an exquisite singing voice. Her name was Agathe von Siebold and she was the daughter of a university professor in Göttengen. Brahms spent many hours with her in the Grimm home, accompanying her while she sang his songs. Their mutual affection became obvious to everyone in the household—especially to Clara Schumann, who was also a frequent house guest there. Although she had often insisted that Brahms should find a nice young woman and marry her, when faced with the actual possibility of anyone taking away "her Johannes," Clara became terribly upset. Brahms tried to avoid conflict by spending time with Clara and her children, but his growing love for Agathe was impossible to disguise. One day on an outing, Clara discovered Brahms with his arm around the young girl's waist. Hurriedly packing up all five children, Clara left Göttingen the same night. Brahms stayed the rest of the summer, but wrote to Clara often offering reassurance of his continuing friendship.

After he returned to the Detmold court in September of 1858, Brahms and Agathe wrote constantly. He sent her new songs and duets, and a choral Bridal Song that he would later destroy. By 1859, he had returned to Göttingen to see her and secretly exchange engagement rings.

Their friends were ecstatic and waited for the public announcement of this ideal match. But it was not to happen. Brahms' Piano Concerto in D minor premiered to hisses and boo's in Leipzig, and his belief in his musical future was shaken. His dark emotional history of sexual abuse continued to make it extremely difficult for him to have a healthy relationship with a woman his own age. And always, his deep attachment to Clara made the idea of marriage to any other woman difficult. All of these factors worked together to make marriage to Agathe an impossibility. He wrote, "I love you! but I cannot wear fetters!" Agathe was proud, took him at his word, and refused to see him again. It would be more than 10 years before she married someone else, and even as an old woman she would still remember Brahms with a sense of deep loss.

Brahms was saddened by the episode, but convinced himself he was destined for the life of a bachelor. In his later days, he carried on brief romances, more often than not with singers, but he never again became emotionally entangled. The only long-standing relationships he maintained were with unattainable, married women who were usually years his senior.

At the end of 1859, Brahms resigned the court appointment in Detmold and made his home in Hamburg, hoping he would be chosen to succeed the aging conductor of the Hamburg Philharmonic Orchestra. In February he conducted the group in the first public performance of his A major Serenade. The D minor Concerto gradually gained acceptance, but it was a huge, uncompromising work that demanded as much energy from its performer and its audience as an average symphony. The critics were not kind.

In the fall of 1862, Brahms left Hamburg for a visit to Vienna. He fell in love with the warm, lovely city filled with coffee houses and gypsy tunes. The openness and generosity of the Viennese was altogether different from the restraint and reserve of Northern Germany. He walked the boulevards with old friends, made many new acquaintances in the city's large musical community, and kept postponing his return date. Instead of just staying a few weeks, he lingered in Vienna through the winter and into the spring.

There was now even less reason to return to Hamburg; the orchestra director's post he had so hoped to receive had instead been given to his good friend Julius Stockhausen. Brahms stayed on in Vienna. He studied some Schubert manuscripts he discovered, presented several solo concerts and worked with an assistant to Richard Wagner in preparing the orchestration of *Die Meistersinger* for a concert Wagner presented in January. Finally, in May of 1863, he left Vienna. On the way back to Hamburg, Brahms stopped to visit his friend Joachim and meet the violinist's fiance, Amalie Weiss. She was a brilliant young opera singer who was retiring from the stage in favor of a concert career. Brahms and Amalie became instant friends and musical partners, and she would soon become a major interpreter of his vocal works.

May 7, 1863 was Johannes Brahms' thirtieth birthday. He returned to Hamburg just in time to celebrate with his family. But the situation at home was wretched. His mother was 74 and an invalid. His father, who preferred the local night life to chores around the house, left most of the responsibility for nursing his wife to Brahms' sister, Elise. Brahms' brother, Fritz, had no interest in holding down a job if someone else could be induced to pay the bills. All four family members looked to Brahms for financial and emotional support. The prospect of living in the same household with them seemed bleak. When a letter came from Vienna offering him the post of conductor for a choral society called the *Singakademie*, Brahms accepted immediately and prepared to move to Vienna. After spending a few days with Clara Schumann in her new summer home in the Black Forest, he headed south.

During the 1862-63 season, he taught in Vienna and directed the *Singakademie* chorus. The group liked his work well enough to re-elect him for a three-year term, but Brahms disliked the job's administrative burden and resigned.

Returning to Hamburg, he found that things at home had deteriorated even further. His brother was doing well now as a piano teacher and had moved out to live in grander style—though he didn't seem able to contribute anything to his mother's upkeep. The parents' marriage had completely deteriorated and the elder Brahms wanted to live alone. Although he was by no means wealthy, Brahms was determined to support both his parents and his sister. He moved his father into lodgings, found a nicer apartment with a garden for his mother and sister, and paid for everything. Exhausted and nearly broke, Brahms headed back to the Black Forest to be with Clara. Combining composing and games of hide-and-seek with Clara's children, he completed his F minor Piano Quintet and wrote the majority of a new String Sextet in G major. These works show Brahms' music at his best—complex, rich, dense and demanding.

In January of 1865, his mother died of a stroke. It was a terrible blow to Brahms, who had loved his mother deeply. His only comfort was work, so he began a major new composition which he called the *German Requiem*. Not a traditional Catholic requiem mass, it was instead a non-traditional form, set to texts Brahms chose from the Lutheran Bible. The verses were messages of comfort to the grieving son. He turned to the *Requiem* for solace many times in the next year. It was to become his largest and most magnificent work.

Wandering around Europe, Brahms performed constantly, trying to earn the necessary money to support his father and sister. He had little time to compose, although he did spend part of the summer writing the sad, painfully beautiful Horn Trio. Finally, he completed the *Requiem* and began to prepare it for pubic performance.

On Good Friday 1868, the elite of the European musical establishment gathered inside Bremen cathedral. Musical director Karl Martin Reinthaler made final preparations with the orchestra, choir and soloists. Johannes Brahms stood at the door of the cathedral, waiting. Moments before the performance was scheduled to begin, a coach pulled up before the great building. From it stepped Clara Schumann and her eldest daughter, Marie. Clara was 48 years old and growing stout. Her face was tired, reflecting the fatigue of the English tour she had completed only days before. But Brahms had needed her to be there, writing:

If only you could be a listener on Good
Friday, I should be more happy than I can say.
It would be as good as half the performance for
me.

She could not have stayed away. With Clara on his
arm, Brahms walked proudly into the cathedral.

The performance was a triumph. Critical response
was excellent and within three weeks, Reinthaler repeated the performance in response to overwhelming
public demand. After some further enlargement and
refinements, the final version of the *Requiem* was heard
in Leipzig, London, more than 20 German and Swiss cities,
Vienna, St. Petersburg and Paris. No other work did more
to win international recognition for Brahms. His reputation as Germany's finest young composer grew.

In 1869, Brahms made his last formal appearances as
a touring concert pianist and decided to move to Vienna.
The death of his father from liver cancer had cut many of
his ties with Hamburg, and now he would make his home
in the Austrian capital.

Vienna was happy to welcome Brahms, and he was
soon offered the post of artistic adviser and conductor to
the *Gesellschaft der Musikfreunde (Society of the Friends*
of Musik). The society sponsored a 300-member choir and
a full symphony orchestra with high professional standards. They gave Brahms complete creative freedom, a
generous salary and the power to hire the best musicians
in Vienna. His three seasons as director of the *Society* are
among the most memorable in its long history. After three
years, he decided that his extensive duties were keeping
him from serious composition and he resigned his direc-
torship, remaining as an honorary director.

For all his success as a composer, Brahms had still not
achieved the major goal of his musical life, a symphony.

He had begun several and discarded them as inadequate. The ghost of Beethoven's great symphonic work haunted him and he didn't feel his work measured up to that impossible standard. But when he finally completed the massive First Symphony is 1876, the results were worth the wait. Pianist and conductor Hans von Bülow, speaking as an admirer not a critic, called Brahms' first symphony "Beethoven's Tenth," because it carried on Beethoven's tradition so effectively. The work was heroic, noble and very much outside the mainstream of his own time. Huge, difficult to relax and enjoy, it was music that demanded a great deal from its listener. The score was dense and heavily instrumented, causing one conductor to look at the orchestration and note, "No light will ever shine in there."

On October 24, 1878, in the Gewandhaus where she made her public debut, Clara Schumann gave her final professional performance. The entire hall was decorated with green and gold wreaths and garlands of oak leaves. As she entered, the audience stood and a rain of flowers began, threatening to completely bury her and her piano. For her last concert she chose Robert Schumann's immortal Concerto in A minor for Piano and Orchestra. It was a long time before she could seat herself at the piano and begin the program. Almost overcome, she began to shake violently. But then, as always, the music was more powerful than the emotion. With masterful control, she played the concerto with perfect calm. In the audience, as always, was her dear friend Johannes.

Throughout the 1870s and 1880s, Brahms continued to compose works of exceptional power and depth. Three more symphonies, another masterful piano concerto, a movingly beautiful double concerto for violin and cello, overtures, chamber music and hundreds of songs for voice and choir, all poured from his pen. But before they went to the publisher, they always went to Clara. Each piece he completed was sent to her first for review, although he sometimes ignored her opinions. Clara considered his success partly her responsibility, for she had spent many years promoting his piano compositions through her concerts. She was extremely happy to see Brahms receive fame and wealth.

Though the two old friends often quarreled during their 43 year friendship, their loyalty remained unshakable. In the last years of their lives, their frequent letters shine with deeply felt affection. In 1895, when the 76-year-old Clara suffered a series of strokes, Brahms wrote and asked Marie:

> *When you believe that the worst may be expected, be so kind as to send word to me so that I can come and still see those dear eyes—those eyes that, when they finally close, will close so much for me.*

On May 20, 1896, Clara died at her home in Frankfurt. Johannes Brahms stood in the rain as they buried her next to their beloved Robert. Eleven months later, Brahms died at the age of 63. In Hamburg, all the ships in the harbor flew their flags at half mast.

THE
SECOND
TRIO

FRANZ LISZT
COSIMA LISZT WAGNER
RICHARD WAGNER

BEAUTIFUL BABY

*How extraordinarily he plays, daringly and madly,
and again tenderly and sweetly—I have heard it all.
But his world is not mine. Art as you practice it, and
as I often do at the piano when composing, this fine
inwardness I would not give up for all his magnifi-
cence—and there is some, too much tinsel with it all.*

—Robert Schumann on Franz Liszt

Four years before his death in 1827, Beethoven came out of self-imposed exile to attend a concert by an 11-year-old prodigy named Franz Liszt. The young pianist was a pale, thin boy who looked so weak Beethoven feared he might collapse at any moment. His face was angelic and he smiled at the audience with a winning sweetness. But when he played, his power was astonishing. Even the deaf old composer could feel the vibrations from the giant piano as it shook and shuddered under the boy's hands. Beethoven made no secret of the fact that he hated most child prodigies, but he came and paid homage. Liszt had made another conquest.

Franz Liszt was a remarkable man, torn apart by two radically different urges. He was a consummate show-man, thriving on the adoration of audiences and triggering frenzied responses whenever he performed. And yet he was also a painfully private person who felt an irresistible urge to withdraw from the public and discover his own private world of musical composition and religious contemplation. The tension between those two sides of his personality marked his entire life, public and private.

Liszt's father, Adam, was a frustrated musician, stuck in the small Hungarian village of Raiding, dreaming of the musical career he would never have. His son Franz was born in 1811, and the young child's tremendous musical talent soon became obvious. By the age of three, the boy had begun to demonstrate remarkable skill as a pianist and a composer. His father immediately recognized Franz's genius as a way out of Hungary—and into the big time.

Liszt was first taught by his father, who played the piano and the cello. He quickly learned everything Adam Liszt could teach him and the time was right to move on to bigger and better things. His father's employer, Prince Esterhazy, was noted as a supporter of the arts. He had been the patron of Joseph Haydn and other fine court musicians of an earlier era. Now, he agreed to sponsor young Liszt in a concert that would launch his career and introduce him to the world of aristocratic patronage. As a result of the concert, Franz (or more accurately, Franz's father) collected a subscription for 600 florins per year. It was enough to support the entire family, and so they moved to Vienna where the boy could continue his education with the era's finest teachers. He studied with Antonio Salieri, Mozart's old rival, for theory and composition, and with Karl Czerny for piano technique. Czerny's exercise books are still around to torment young musicians, probably because young Liszt learned his lessons so well he guaranteed Czerny's place in the history of musical education.

In Vienna of the 1820's, musicians found their popular audiences in the salons of the rich. Brilliant and ambitious ladies, many of whom were wives of wealthy Jewish merchants, put together the best and the brightest of the city's artistic types in glittering parties. Music was performed, poetry read and great ideas tossed around freely, along with idle gossip. By the age of 12, Liszt had learned to charm the pants off of these adoring ladies. It was a skill he put to use often, especially with the eager young women who constantly surrounded him. The beautiful boy was adored and spoiled in the salons of Vienna. His next capital to conquer was Paris.

Liszt took Paris by storm. By age twelve, after a triumphal tour of Germany, Franz Liszt became the newest darling of the French salons. At an age when Robert Schumann and Richard Wagner were still staging amateur theatricals with their grade school friends, Liszt was an international sensation.

For the next four years Liszt worked constantly. He performed for the crowned heads of France and England, playing in recitals and salons across Europe. But the exploitation and constant public exposure exhausted the young performer. By age 16, the child star was worn out.

Adam Liszt's sudden death that year changed the agenda. Free from the pressure to perform, young Franz withdrew from society. Without his father to push him, he did not want to stay in the spotlight. He was emotionally empty.

He gave piano lessons to support his mother and pay off his father's debts, but Liszt refused to perform. He fell in love with a pupil, Carolyn de Saint-Criq. Her mother had been a patron of Liszt, hiring him to teach her lovely daughter. But Carolyn's father was not impressed with the young musician. When her mother died, Carolyn's father married her off to the Count d'Artigaux without asking Carolyn or Franz. More than 30 years later, Liszt still remembered her with sentiment in his will.

Romantic disappointment—not something he was used to—made him withdraw even further. For the next 18 months, deeply depressed, he suffered from a series of psychosomatic illness and rumors of his death circulated around Paris. A devout Catholic, Liszt seriously considered taking vows in the church at this time, but his priest talked him out of it, telling him to find God in music, which was his natural gift.

To bring himself out of his depression, Liszt began reading widely. Almost entirely self-educated, because the life of the child prodigy doesn't lend itself well to formal education, he now began to study everything he could get his hands on—religion, history, fiction and poetry.

All that reading broadened his horizons and opened up a mind that had been narrowly focused on his music for too long. When he came out of his cave, Liszt began looking around. Political liberalism was everywhere and it was exhilarating. The revolution of 1830 filled the streets of Paris with gunfire and Liszt was swept away by the radical new ideas of political, artistic and religious freedom. His mother said, "The guns cured him."

Liszt was back—with a vengeance. Filled with musical excitement by the performances of Berlioz, Chopin and the great violin virtuoso Paganini, he began to completely rethink his approach to the piano and to improve his already brilliant technique through thousands of hours of practice. After seeing a performance by Paganini, whose gaunt, cadaverous face, burning eyes and sinister reputation had taken Paris by storm in 1831, Liszt caught fire. Obsessively determined to match Paganini's virtuosity with his own, he turned the heat on for his own audiences. His composition *Fantasy on a Paganini's La Clochette* and his piano transcription of Berlioz's *Symphonie Fantastique* were astonishingly difficult, unplayable by anyone but him, and the rage of Paris. Composing virtuoso works that showed off one's talent was a common tool of showmanship at the time, and Liszt made good use of the technique.

BEAUTIFUL BABY

During 1831 and 1832, Liszt was joined in Paris by a crowd of gifted young musicians, including Berlioz, Chopin, Mendelssohn and a 14-year-old prodigy named Clara Schumann, who stunned Paris audiences with her musical skill.

Liszt's audiences were responsive, especially the beautiful women who gathered around his dressing room door. Liszt was never shy with them. He took what he liked and he saw a lot that he liked. He moved through a series of love affairs, some lasting months, some only minutes.

But in early 1831, he met a woman whose life was to be tied intimately together with his own for more than a decade. At an elegant soiree hosted by the Marquise le Vayer, he caught the eye of the Countess Marie d'Agoult, the next great love of his life. Was she a devil or an angel? It depends on who you ask. She was undoubtedly brilliant, wealthy, passionate and powerful, with a violent temper and great talent as an author.

She had inherited wealth from her mother, royal ancestors from her father, and by the time she met Liszt, she had also acquired a boring, frustrating marriage in the classic French style.

Marie described herself as "six inches of snow over twenty feet of lava."

There is no question that she genuinely loved Liszt, but their relationship was stormy. When they met she was 28 and he was 22. They both recognized an immediate attraction—intellectual and physical. She was overwhelmed by Liszt's genius. He was impressed with her social position, although she was a little embarrassed by it. They began a passionate, chaotic love affair of almost blinding intensity. It was difficult from the start. Even the earliest months of their relationship were marked with constant fights, jealousy, passionate demands and emotional blackmail.

Marie's arrangement with the Count d'Agoult had become a marriage of convenience. She and Liszt openly spent time together in her luxurious country home. For the first year of their relationship, it was simply a traditional affair. But then she did something that broke all the rules of convention. After the emotional shock of her eldest daughter's death, Marie sent her four-year-old daughter Claire to boarding school and left her husband to join Liszt in Switzerland. She was pregnant, and the baby was Liszt's.

There was a great difference in how the 19th Century world treated a man and a woman in an adulterous relationship. Moral misdemeanors could be ignored in a man, especially when he was a tremendously popular musician. But they meant social doom for a woman. For two months, the lovers traveled alone and were happy and serene. But when they settled in Switzerland and Liszt again became the center of public attention, Marie quickly felt the sting of public blame. When the world broke in to continue its adoration of Liszt, she was excluded and their relationship began the long and painful process of falling apart.

Marie settled in Switzerland, developing the popularity of her writing with magazine articles published under the name of Daniel Stern, and waited for their baby. Blandine was born on December 18, 1835.

Money was a constant problem. Cut off from family money, Marie's remaining personal income was not enough to support them both. Liszt, caught up in the pleasures of romance, hadn't performed for two years, and he needed money to support his mother. So in April of 1836, he took off to do a series of concerts in Lyon, France. Faithfully promising Marie he wouldn't go to Paris, he immediately went to Paris.

She was not pleased.

Liszt, on the other hand, was having a great time. He socialized with Chopin, entertained popular composer Giacomo Meyerbeer and saw Meyerbeer's hugely successful opera *Robert le Diable (Robert the Devil)*. Meyerbeer had introduced his first grand opera the year before. Giacomo Meyerbeer, whose mother actually named him Jakob Liebmann Beer, was admittedly a complete musical opportunist. He was never ashamed that he wrote strictly to please the masses. When he went to Italy, he changed his name to Giacomo and wrote better opera than most Italians. When he went to France, he became the most charming of Frenchmen, and wrote grand French opera. Robert Schumann disliked Meyerbeer's music because he thought it was shallow and superficial. Wagner hated Meyerbeer because he was a Jew who was hugely successful at a time when Wagner couldn't find an audience. Wagner's personal prejudices aside, Meyerbeer's music had pretty easy virtue. *Robert le Diable* featured a ballet of dead nuns rising from their graves to dance among monastery ruins at midnight. It offered just enough scandalous eroticism to make it a huge success, and it kept making money for the next 25 years. Meyerbeer was a gracious man, liked and respected by his peers—even those who didn't like his music. It's no surprise that the man whose music had the singular distinction of being disliked *both* by Wagner and Schumann attracted the friendship of Franz Liszt.

Liszt didn't go back to Switzerland until July. In the meantime, Marie stayed home with the new baby, growing angry, frustrated and jealous. The next time Liszt went to Paris, Marie went along, leaving the baby, Blandine, with a nurse.

Liszt went to Paris for a showdown with his arch rival, the famous keyboard athlete Sigismund Thalberg. This world series of piano playing would decide, once and for all, who was Europe's ultimate virtuoso. During Liszt's two-year absence, Thalberg's reputation had begun to outshine his own, and Liszt was determined to even the score. The final showdown came at a deadly serious soirée hosted by the Princess Belgiojoso. Liszt came out swinging, dazzled the audience with impossible skill, tossed his magnificent mane of hair and contorted his face into expressions of artistic agony. When the piece was finished, he collapsed into the arms of a bystander— unconscious. Someone said he looked like Christ crucified, although he conveniently recovered moments later. It was no contest. Liszt was the winner by acclamation.

In addition to his absolute domination of the keyboard, Liszt was beginning to establish his reputation as a composer. He was a raging hurricane when he played the piano, overwhelming his audience with an almost diabolical strength at the keyboard, and his piano compositions capture that strength and skill. As his musical understanding grew, his compositions began to move beyond being virtuoso vehicles designed only to show off his technique. Liszt created exotic new harmonies and original forms that can be considered serious contributions to the development of modern music. Some of his most memorable original piano works included the massive B minor Sonata, Etudes and Nocturnes, the *Mephisto Waltzes*, Rhapsodies and a series of musical travelogues called the *Années de Pele'rinage*. His output for piano was huge and included hundreds of piano transcriptions of operas and symphonies.

Liszt wrote for orchestra as well as piano. He specialized in what we now call "program" music, music that depicted stories and ideas rather than just the abstracts of "absolute" music, that described only themselves. *Les Preludes* are a series of symphonic poems that reflect the ideas of French philosopher Lamartine.

Mazepa graphically depicts the wild ride across the steppes of a mythical Cossack hero of the same name. Liszt also wrote two piano concerti for piano and orchestra that remain the ultimate display of virtuoso technique for any serious pianist. Their technical difficulty and brilliant display were equaled by his *Hungarian Fantasy* for Piano and Orchestra, which was constructed around tunes reminiscent of the home country Liszt never really knew. His most ambitious orchestral work was the *Faust* Symphony, which depicts the three principal character's from Goethe's epic poem.

By 1837 Marie was pregnant again, so she and Liszt headed off for another romantic period of isolation, this time on Italy's Lake Como. They were both happy during these quiet periods, when Liszt could resist the siren's call of fame and his female fans, and Marie had him all to herself. Marie didn't share well—and Liszt had an extremely hard time sticking to the subject. Their daughter Cosima was born on December 26, 1837.

In March of 1838, Liszt took Marie to Venice and left her. He went on to Vienna, alone. There, he continued a lifelong practice of trotting out his "bag of tricks." These were programs that contained healthy doses of theatrics, pleased his audiences and were financially successful. They were roughly equivalent to modern professional wrestling, stage-managed to include broken strings and ladies fainting in the audience. Sometimes the constant battle for audience approval left Liszt feeling a little cheap. He wrote, "Am I condemned for my life to amuse in drawing rooms?" Yet he chose to continue in the style he had always depended on for easy results.

But there was much more to his talent than cheap theatrics, even if he did rely on them far too often. His performances in Vienna were masterful, and he set off an absolute frenzy in his audiences. Since childhood, Liszt had known huge popularity, but even for him, the response in Vienna was amazing. One happy result was the artistic freedom which popularity gave him. He could play anything he chose, and he began to choose well. Schumann, Chopin, Mendelssohn, and always— Beethoven. The greatest musicians in Europe were in Vienna to see him, including a 19-year-old Clara Wieck, whose popularity in Vienna equalled his own.

While Liszt was the center of attention in Vienna, Marie was miserable. Feeling abandoned in Venice, she worked herself into a state of physical illness. She sent off an anguished letter to Liszt in Vienna, begging him to come back. He did not return, though he asked her to come to Vienna. Knowing she would be shunned in Austria, and unwilling to bend her stubborn pride, she refused. After more bitter quarrels, Marie suggested a separation. It was Liszt's turn to refuse. They stayed together for another year, traveling around Italy trying to recapture their lost love. A third child, Daniel, was born in Rome on May 9, 1839. In the autumn of that year, she returned to Paris and Liszt set off on an extensive tour of Europe. Although their final parting was still five years away, this was the beginning of the end for their love affair.

The return to Paris had been suggested by Marie's brother, who was ready to accept her with one small condition—the children had to disappear. She didn't object, and Liszt encouraged her to do anything that would help her get reestablished in French society, and out of his hair.

It was not likely she would miss the children, for she barely knew them. In keeping with the custom among wealthy folks, the babies had been placed with different nurses soon after their births; Blandine in Switzerland and Cosima in Italy. Blandine joined her parents when she turned three and had never even met her younger sister. Marie collected the one-year-old Cosima from her nurse and deposited both girls with Liszt's mother in Paris. Daniel remained safely in Italy with his nurse.

Anna Liszt was a warm and loving grandmother, and the two girls were fortunate to have her care. Their mother was soon engrossed in rebuilding her social life and writing career. She rarely saw the children, though they lived near her in Paris.

Marie and Liszt were separated ten months a year, she working on her writing, he on an almost endless tour of the continent. But their final split was still to come. During vacations, they would travel together and try to regain their lost romance. It was a losing battle—and often a noisy one. Their loud quarrels inevitably focused on Marie's jealousy.

She had a lot to be jealous about. Liszt collected lovers on his concert tours the way other tourists picked up souvenir post cards. Women threw themselves at the great star, and he was always willing to catch them. In the spring of 1844, Marie made the final break. She no longer wanted to see him, speak to him or write to him.

When their parents finally ended their unofficial union, Blandine was already beautiful and her mother's favorite. Cosima was the ugly duckling, with a serious nature and a big nose. Cosima was usually left behind when her mother took Blandine out on their rare holidays. Daniel, the baby son, was picked up from the nurse, deposited with Grandma, and then completely ignored by both parents.

Liszt left Paris and Marie, anxious to put all traces of the relationship behind him. He would not see the children or Paris again for another nine years. His anger at Marie began to grow, and he decided to get even by taking away her children. After first legally legitimizing them, a step he had never bothered to take before, he went to court and was granted total custody. Marie was completely forbidden to visit or see them. She fought, but it was a largely hopeless case under the legal system of the time. And in truth, although losing custody was a blow since she had rarely seen them before, one wonders how deeply affected she actually was.

Liszt would not let Marie visit the children, but he didn't visit them himself, either. He wrote infrequently, sometimes only once every three months, which is difficult to understand in a person who frequently wrote six letters a day. The children were crushed by their separation from their mother. Although they had seen her infrequently, contact with her was the only parental love they received. They wrote to Liszt begging for permission to write their mother. They were forbidden to even speak of her.

Clinging to each other for support, the three children lived a sad, lonely life, abandoned by both parents. Their only comfort was Grandmother Liszt.

The two eldest girls eventually went to boarding school, while Daniel stayed with their grandmother. All three children received an excellent education and were serious about their studies, which included Greek and Latin, modern languages, history, literature and music. Cosima especially excelled at music, becoming an excellent pianist and composer. Her secret goal, she later revealed in her diaries, was to play the piano so well her father would respect her and pay her some attention. Of all the children, Cosima most worshiped her father and most keenly felt the pain of his abandonment.

Liszt, meanwhile, was crossing the continent playing Chopin, Weber, Schubert and catching flowers thrown from the audience by interested ladies. In Kiev, he met a lady very different from any he had ever been seduced by—the Princess Carolyn Sayn-Wittgenstein.

The Princess was a Polish aristocrat with a brilliant mind, an iron will and an addiction to cigars. She was not beautiful, but her flashing black eyes were astonishingly intense. She had been married to the Prince Nicholas Sayn-Wittgenstein at 17. Now, at age 28, she was separated from her husband and living on one of her estates near Kiev.

It was love at first sight, and the effect on Liszt was earthshaking. She met his deep psychological need in some unexplained way we will never understand. Whatever the reason, she owned him—and she was convinced he needed her to run his life. She set about the task with a powerful will.

In 1842, the Grand Duke of Saxe-Weimar-Eisenach had appointed Liszt as Special Musical Director (Kapellmeister) of the capital city of Weimar. Since 1842 Liszt had been spending three months a year in Goethe's home town, where the Grand Duke was a royal patron in the old style who prided himself in supporting the finest artistic courtiers. In 1848, with revolution sweeping Europe, Weimar looked like a relatively safe place to set up housekeeping. One month before his thirty-sixth birthday, Liszt made his last commercial performance and retired from the stage. He was determined to lead a quieter life, devoting himself to composing and conducting. He returned to Weimar with the Princess and her daughter, Marie, following close behind. He found a house for them and checked into a hotel for two weeks. He then abandoned all pretense and moved in with her.

The Princess was a devout Catholic and not pleased about the idea of living in sin, but it was difficult for her to marry Liszt when she already had a husband. As a Catholic, a religious ceremony was essential to her good conscience, but being married in the church was not possible after a civil divorce, so the Princess began the long, exhausting process of trying to get an annulment.

She had excellent grounds, having been married at 17, essentially against her will—or at least without her informed consent. Normally, it would have been easily done. But this was a highly political situation, not just a religious matter. It was also a serious economic question. If her annulment were granted, the Prince might be forced to return her dowry and lose access to her huge fortune. Money and politics brought some of the aristocracy's biggest guns into the action. The Princess had counted on the Grand Duchess of Weimar to convince the Czar of Russia (the Duchess' brother) to ask for approval of the annulment. But the Prince brought his own artillery to bear on the Czar's court. The Sayn-Wittgenstein family was enormously wealthy and equally influential with the Czar. He not only refused to grant approval for the annulment, he turned around and confiscated all the Princess's property, giving half to her husband and keeping half in trust for daughter Marie.

The fallout from the Czar's decision was ugly, and it eventually extended all the way to the children in Paris. In Weimar, the Princess immediately ran out of money and social position. The local gentry took her off all the good invitation lists. She was now completely dependent on Liszt for financial support and social interaction. They grew closer and more paranoid, surrounded by a world full of real and imagined enemies.

Marie d'Agoult confirmed their worst fears by publishing a vicious little roman à clef called *Nelida*. It was a classic kiss-and-tell romance novel that made her look like a plaster saint and Liszt look like a complete idiot. Liszt was livid. The Princess was outraged.

It became a season of revenge.

Liszt took out his spite, not on Marie, but on his own children. Learning that they had defied his wishes and visited their mother, he abruptly pulled them from school and ordered them back to his mother's home under strict supervision. The children had been so audacious as to go see Marie—and then, being the dutiful children they were, had immediately written and confessed all to their father. This treason was unforgivable to Liszt, who demanded absolute loyalty and absolute obedience. Cosima was devastated at being forced to leave her friends and her school. She wrote dozens of tearful, pleading letters, begging forgiveness and pleading to be reunited with her adored friend, Mlle. Laure. This kind lady, sister of their school director, had been a second mother to Cosima—or more accurately a first mother, the original having been notably absent. But Liszt would not relent. And he wasn't finished.

He and the Princess had their ultimate revenge in the person of Madame Patersi de Fossombroni. This ancient lady was the drill sergeant disciplinarian who had, when the Princess was a teenager, whipped her into shape. The girls were to be removed, not only from school, but now even from their grandmother's home, and placed in the care of Madame Patersi and her sister. Once again tearful letters were piled into the mail, but Liszt (or more accurately, the Princess) could not be convinced to change his mind.

From this day forward throughout her young life, Cosima's relationship with her father was filtered through the glass of Princess Caroline's jealousy. The Princess opened all mail, censored its contents and answered Liszt's letters. Her decisions about the children's lives were final. They were always couched in terms of what was best for their father's honor and his needs, and they were always obeyed.

In 1853, Liszt returned to Paris. It was the first time he had seen his children in almost 10 years. At age 43, his great wild hair had turned iron gray. His once soft and lovely face was no longer youthful, it had hardened into severe grimness. That October, he brought a small party with him to Paris: The Princess, her beautiful and spoiled 18-year-old daughter Marie, and their devoted friend, Richard Wagner.

The young Princess, Marie, remembered the event in her own especially vicious style.

> *I was older than the two girls who were still rather unpolished and who looked out at the unfriendly world with timid doe eyes. The elder, Blandine, was prettier, plumper, more pleasing—though in no way heaven-storming, and she was already rather pleased with herself. Poor Cosima, however, was in the worst teen-age stage—tall and angular, sallow, with a wide mouth and long nose, the image of her father. Only her long golden hair, of unusual sheen, was of great beauty. Her brother Daniel was the youngest—a pale, sad-looking boy with dreamy eyes...After a simple meal Wagner read us the end of the Nibelungen. The children understood scarcely enough German to grasp the meaning of the words. Still, even they were gripped by our emotions. I can still see Cosima's rapturous expression with the tears running down her sharp nose. At that time, Wagner had no eyes for the ugly child.*

Blandine and Cosima's lonely life in Paris was beginning to brighten. After the October visit, the girls were allowed to visit their father in Brussels—without the Princess. It was a warm, affectionate opportunity for the daughters to really get to know their father, perhaps the first they had ever experienced. He was amazed to find them mature, serious and intelligent. He was also extremely impressed with 17-year-old Cosima's great musical talent.

At the same time, the Countess d'Agoult had again entered their lives. No longer able to restrict the children's movements, Liszt had given his grudging permission for them to visit their mother. She was fascinated with her opportunity to shape their young minds and set about giving them a wider education in art and culture. News of her influence on the girls inevitably reached the Princess, setting off a storm of jealousy and anger. Unable to control their contacts in Paris, she was determined to put them out of their mother's reach. She decided that Cosima and Blandine should be moved immediately to Berlin. Her decision, rubber-stamped by Liszt, set off another storm. The Countess was livid, Grandmother Liszt was grief stricken and the girls were crushed. They spoke very little German, knew absolutely no one in Berlin and could not understand why their father would uproot them from everything they knew and everyone they loved in Paris. But the Princess prevailed, and after much sadness, the two young women submitted to their father's wishes and moved to Berlin. They were to live with the mother of Liszt's most devoted student, Hans von Bülow.

The Bülow name was ancient and honorable, but the current generation carrying the name had little but honor to live on. Hans' iron-willed mother had been determined that he would study law and make his fortune. But at age 20, after two unhappy years of dreaming about music while pretending to study law, he set off on foot to find his idol, Richard Wagner, in Zurich. Wagner had been his role model since age twelve, and Hans was eager to study music with him. Bülow's talent impressed Wagner so highly that he was granted a musical apprenticeship as assistant conductor to Wagner in Zurich. Bülow and his friend, Karl Ritter, stayed with Wagner for six months before moving on to Weimar to study with Liszt.

By 1855, when Cosima arrived in Berlin, Bülow's years of apprenticeship were over. He was a respected young conductor and concert pianist, making a name for himself in Berlin. At age 18, Cosima was no longer a shy, awkward girl. She had become a strong-willed and intelligent young woman with a strong sense of her own personal destiny. She believed her destiny was to support the genius of a man who would some day be as great as her father. Bülow encouraged her to begin her own concert career but she was convinced her own abilities were too limited for greatness. He begged Cosima and her father for a chance to introduce her playing in public, but Liszt found the idea impossible and Cosima would never have dreamed of defying him. Throughout her life, she had bent her strong will to his wishes, even when they hurt her deeply. She could not change now, but her times with Bülow during her piano lessons were warm and affectionate, and her skills as a pianist continued to astonish him.

Bülow was a gifted young musician with a brilliant future. Cosima saw in him the potential for genius, and she decided he was the man whose future would be worth her devotion. Hans was stunned that this gifted young woman, daughter of his greatest teacher, would find him worthy. Their courtship lasted for two years and in August of 1857, they were married with Liszt's blessing, although he did not attend the wedding.

The first stop on their honeymoon was Switzerland and the home of Richard Wagner. More than anything in the world, Hans von Bülow wanted Wagner to approve of his young bride.

THE MAKING OF A MAESTRO

...if you heard his operas on the stage, many parts could not but move you deeply. And, if it is not clear sunlight that the genius radiates, it is often, nevertheless, a mysterious magic that overpowers our senses.

—Robert Schumann on Richard Wagner

Richard Wagner's birth was announced by cannons. Napoleon's troops were entrenched near Leipzig, locked in battle with the allied Prussian and Russian armies. Beaten in Russia, Napoleon was making one more try on Berlin. Leipzig lay directly in his path. Although the city had no strategic value, it was witnessing one of the final, decisive battles of the Napoleonic wars. In the streets of the Saxon city the sound of guns could be heard day and night. On May 21, 1813, the fields around Leipzig were thick with cannon smoke and littered with the bodies of the dead. The next day, Richard Wagner was born.

His mother, Johanna, may have been the illegitimate daughter of Prince Constantin of Saxe-Weimar-Eisenach—or she may have been his lover before her marriage—it depends on which historical researcher one believes.

His father may have been Carl Friedrich Wagner, a police official and amateur actor with a predilection for young actresses—or it may have been Friedrich's best friend, Ludwig Geyer. Once again, the record is a little vague.

The battles around Leipzig continued throughout the summer, leading to a final French victory in October. Friedrich Wagner died in the typhus epidemic that followed the war. Richard Wagner was six months old.

Geyer was a portrait painter and actor in a traveling theatrical troop. After Friederich's death, he married Johanna and took on the responsibility of supporting her seven children. Another child, Cäcilie, was born to them five months later. The family moved to Dresden, where Geyer performed in the Court Theater. He was the only father Richard knew, and the boy called himself Richard Geyer until he was 14.

Richard made his stage debut the week after his second birthday. He appeared in a special stage production with original music by Carl Maria von Weber. Pale and sickly, he had a thin little body almost too small to support his abnormally large head. Richard was sewn into tights with wings on his back and gracefully posed as an angel. His father, Ludwig, looked on affectionately. Geyer was a kind and affectionate father to the rambunctious little boy he called the Cossack. When the performance was over, he gave the young actor an iced cake and told him it was from the King, whose return from exile was the occasion the show celebrated.

The Wagner/Geyers were a theatrical family. Albert, the eldest son, became an excellent operatic tenor, often managing to find musical jobs for Richard in his theatrical companies. Rosalie debuted as an actress under Geyer and joined the Dresden court theater. Luise was an actress in Breslau. Klara was to become a gifted opera singer, successful throughout Germany.

At age seven, Richard was sent away from home for the first of many times. There are numerous hints in his autobiography, *Mein Leben*, of his mother's lack of affection and warmth during his childhood. He recalled:

The anxieties and pressures of bringing up a large family (of which I was the seventh living member), the difficulties in obtaining all we needed, and at the same time satisfying, despite her very limited means, a certain inclination for ostentation, robbed her of that warm tone of motherly tenderness for her family; I can hardly ever remember being cuddled by her, in fact there were never any displays of tenderness in our family...

In 1821 Geyer died, leaving Richard fatherless again at the age of eight. His mother depended on the income of her singing and acting children, so she moved away with them. She sent Richard on a series of shuffles that moved him around from home to home through a number of willing relatives. Whenever family finances were tight, his mother sent him away to live with friends or family.

The next year marked the death of Napoleon and the birth of modern German Opera. Richard's greatest hero was the great operatic composer, Carl Maria von Weber. The nine-year-old boy watched him walk by the window every day on his way to the new opera house. When Weber's great and innovative new opera, *Der Freischütz*, premiered that year, it was received with great approval all over Germany. Not the least of his new fans was Richard, who built props, made costumes and endlessly acted out scenes from the opera, pressing all his friends into service as supporting actors and audience. His cousin remembered one such performance:

At that time the boy's whole mind was full of Der Freischütz—*one example among many will prove this. Among other things Richard had a theater in his room. As soon as he had seen Der Freischütz, he had to put it on immediately. It was—naturally—the scene in the wolf's glen that the boy felt was most suitable. So out came the papiér maché and the glue in order to produce the necessary equipment. His schoolfriends had to join in the work. Scenery and curtains, fireworks and animals—everything was produced; my mother particularly admired a great boar, which was rolled in on a plank looking with its fearful tusks horribly like the Prince of Hell in person. The performance was to be staged at a friend's. Richard played Caspar, but Max hadn't learned his part, and when Richard whispered his disapproval he at first laughed, then swore. And the others laughed and jeered, too.*

When not acting out his private fantasies at home, he was an indifferent student—rough, unruly and often rude to his teachers. His favorite subterfuge was charging candy to his mother's account at the local store without her knowing.

At age 13, he began studying music. Although he never mastered an instrument, he continued to be fascinated by composition and by writing plays. His first dramatic effort was *Leubald*—a mixture of *Macbeth* and *Hamlet* filled with ghosts and multiple murders. In it, he killed off 44 characters and was forced to bring most of them back as ghosts so he would have somebody left in the fourth act.

Unhappy at school and missing the company of his sisters and mother, Richard came up with a scheme that would let him join them in their new home town of Leipzig. He lied to school officials, telling them his mother had sent for him, and walked all the way to Leipzig. Once his presence there was established, his family agreed to let him stay and enrolled him in classes.

Richard loved the life of Leipzig and its university atmosphere. He never attended classes, but gloried in the drinking, gambling and gang activity of the student clubs. His major activities were dueling, hanging around on street corners and designing special costumes for secret societies to which he belonged. The climax of his student career was in 1830, when the July Revolution in Paris lead to restlessness in Leipzig. University students sang and marched in the streets and a drunken Wagner joined in the frenzied ransacking of a brothel. He woke up the next morning with a piece of torn red curtain in his hand and a bad hangover. "That morning," he claims in his memoirs, "I decided I had better devote my life to art, or I would end up dead within a year."

The first result of his new devotion was an Overture in B flat major, scored in red, green and black ink to indicate the spiritual mood of each theme. Through his family's connections with the Gewandhaus conductor, he managed to get the Overture included in the Christmas day concert. Unfamiliar as he was with orchestral scoring, Richard had tried some interesting and inventive new effects. Unfortunately, they involved the rhythmic and unexpected drumming of the timpani through the entire piece. At first the audience was aghast, then they began to laugh. Each time the drum boomed out, they laughed louder. Thankful that his name had not been listed on the program, he snuck away in shame, forever remembering the pitying look on the doorman's face.

Richard enrolled in several schools within Leipzig University. It was required by student club rules that he at least be registered in school in order to participate in club activities. But he never completed a course of study.

This is not to say the boy was dim. He studied voraciously on his own, and was especially in love with German history and ancient mythology.

Made aware of his deficiencies as a composer by the Christmas day concert disaster, Richard decided to study music. He borrowed a book on composition from Friederich Wieck and studied with the choir director of St. Thomas' and other local musicians for three years. In his autobiography, he recalled hearing the great operatic soprano Wilhelmine Schröder-Devrient sing Beethoven's opera *Fidelio* in Leipzig and claimed it as one of his greatest musical inspirations. The only problem with that story is the fact that there is no record of her ever performing *Fidelio* in Leipzig. He probably made up the story to fit his mood many years later when he wrote his autobiography. Wagner had a poetical disregard for the truth if it got in the way of telling a good story. But regardless of the inspiration, his compositions became good enough for performance. A performance of his Symphony in C at the Gewaundhaus prompted Clara Wieck to write Robert Schumann and tell him that Herr Wagner was gaining on him.

At age 20, Richard finally dropped out of school and went to Würzburg to stay with his brother Albert who was singing there in the theater. Leaving town was a necessity in order to avoid heavy gambling debts, the relatives of several young women he had seduced and a large number of angry creditors. Everywhere he went, Wagner left behind mountains of unpaid bills. Albert found him a job as chorus master at Würzburg, where he drilled the chorus for their parts in Meyerbeer's *Robert le Diable.* Here he composed his first complete opera, *Die Feen (The Fairies).* It was never performed in his lifetime.

By the age of 20, Richard had grown a beard and grown into his head, though he remained a small man. His rugged face carried a prominent nose and the scars of an inflammatory skin disease (erysipelas) that was to bother him his whole life. But his less-than-romantic looks didn't stop him from being a constant attraction to beautiful women. His eyes were filled with burning intensity, and his intelligence and powerful personality made him strongly attractive to many people, male and female. His favorite recollection of Würzburg was an afternoon at a country wedding, where he made love to a beautiful young actress named Friederike Galvani in the bushes—while her lover, the oboe player, ran around the country church looking for them.

Soon after, he left Würzburg, perhaps under the encouragement of the oboe player, and took a few months off to write the libretto for another opera, *Das Liebesverbot* (*The Ban on Love*), based on Shakespeare's *Measure for Measure*. In desperate need of money to pay expenses, he decided to consider a job as musical director of Heinrich Bethmann's theater company.

The company was playing a small auditorium in the run-down resort town of Bad Lauchstädt. Bethmann met him on the street outside the theater in his dressing gown and night cap with a three day's growth of beard and a bad hangover. Bethmann's request was absurd. He wanted Wagner to conduct Mozart's *Don Giovanni* the following Sunday, without any rehearsal. Wagner turned on his heel and refused. But he changed his plans when he met the company's leading actress, Minna Planer, at the boarding house where he was staying. She was a 25-year-old black-haired beauty with deep blue eyes and a very attractive walk. He introduced himself to her as the new conductor and went back to tell Bethmann that he would conduct *Don Giovanni* after all.

Minna resisted his advances for two years. She had other lovers and Wagner was in an almost constant state of jealous rage. Finally, the two of them went to a party and got very drunk. He followed her home, fell asleep on her bed, and at dawn, finally talked her into surrender. They became lovers, but she resisted his proposals of marriage.

Minna was shy for good reason. Wagner already had a reputation as a spendthrift and a philanderer. She had been hurt before, and the result of her indiscretion was a young daughter whom everyone believed was her sister. But she could not resist the powerful appeal of this gifted young man, and they traveled together with the company. He became known as a technically good conductor with an exciting performing style popular with singers and audiences.

Wagner's idol, Schröder-Devrient sang several successful concerts with him in April of 1835 and was so impressed by his talent, and his worship of her singing, that she agreed to sing in a benefit performance—for Wagner. He hired a large orchestra, went deeply into debt in anticipation of ticket sales, and decided to perform Beethoven's *Battle* Symphony with double the normal number of brass and deafening array of drums for the cannon. But the auditorium was more than half empty. The public didn't believe such a noted diva was really going to show up—and the ticket prices were very high. Schröder-Devrient sang beautifully, but when the deafening noise of the huge orchestra and the pseudo cannons and muskets shook the empty hall, she left and so did most of the audience. The next morning, a crowd of shouting creditors gathered outside his hotel room, demanding their money. Wagner lost everything on the disastrous concert, but managed to talk his way through the crowd with the help of one woman to whom he owed a large amount, telling them all to send him the bills in Leipzig. He never paid her or anyone else.

Wagner completed *Das Liebesverbot* and performed it with the Bethmann company in Magdeburg in the spring of 1836. The performances lost money and pushed the already financially shaky group over the edge of bankruptcy. Both Wagner and Minna were out of a job. She left to join the Königstad Theater in Berlin. Wagner traveled to several cities trying to find a producer for the opera and eventually joined Minna in Berlin.

On a stormy afternoon in November of 1836, the priest of a small parish outside Berlin opened his door to find two wet people arguing. Minna and Richard had come to arrange a wedding, but their discussion was far from tender. Minna was angry and frightened because they were constantly harassed by creditors. Richard was livid because he was convinced Minna was having an affair. They were married that afternoon. Their relationship immediately fell into a pattern of brutal arguments and mutual abuse followed by pleas for forgiveness.

Five months later, Wagner was appointed musical director of the Königsberg Theater. The company was so broke he frequently had to work without a salary, but he continued to buy expensive clothes and furnishings and give large parties with expensive wine in abundance. Once again, his debt began to grow, and he had absolutely no way to pay for it. Minna left him and went home to her mother. Wagner was convinced she had run away with a shopkeeper. He tracked her down at her parent's home in Dresden. She agreed to return, at least temporarily. But they separated again when he had to sneak out of Königsberg one step ahead of the police and his creditors.

Wagner pursued a post as musical director of the theater in Riga, a Lithuanian town now part of Russia, that had a large German population. It was the last outpost of German civilization in the East, but it was a job. And, he didn't owe anyone in Russia money. Minna wrote to apologize. Wagner invited her to come and live with him in Riga.

Wagner was frustrated by his role in the theater, but he threw himself passionately into composition of his next opera *Rienzi, the Last of the Tribunes*. The melodrama of ancient Rome was based on a novel by the English author Sir Edward Bulwer-Lytton, author of the English language's most infamous opening lines: "It was a dark and stormy night. Suddenly a shot rang out."

By March of 1839, Wagner found himself out of a job again after violent disagreements with the theater's director over the threats of arrest for his growing debts. After leaving a trail of unpaid bills across Germany, he had made a mess of his finances in Russia too. His angry creditors went to court and impounded Wagner's passport. Unable to leave Russia legally, Wagner's friend Abraham Möller helped him arrange an escape.

It was a dark and stormy night on the Russian frontier. Actually, it was a warm August evening. Möller sent his coach to take Richard, Minna and their huge Newfoundland dog, Robber, to the border. They met a friend of Möller near the border who guided them to a smuggler's inn. The main room was filled with Polish Jews who made Wagner very nervous. He hid behind a curtain. Across the road from the inn was a huge ditch that ran the length of the frontier. It was guarded by heavily armed Cossack soldiers with orders to shoot on sight. When the guard changed at midnight, the Wagners and their faithful dog ran into the ditch, scrambled up the other side and out of sight.

The trio huddled in the back of a clumsy oxcart, traveling on back roads to avoid Prussian border guards. The cart hit a rut in a farm yard, threw Wagner into a pile of manure and injured Minna. They spent the night in a peasant's cottage, where Minna had a miscarriage that may have left her unable to have any more children.

Several days rough journey finally brought them to a Baltic port where Möller had arranged passage. Sneaking through high grass to a small dingy, they slipped onto a tiny merchant vessel and hid among the baggage in the hold while port inspectors searched the ship. The crew hoisted Robber up the side of the ship in a cargo net. There followed a horrifying trip to England through huge storms that Wagner later claimed were his inspiration to write *Der fliegende Holländer* (*The Flying Dutchman*).

Their goal was Paris, a center of musical excitement where opera composers were well-paid and Wagner did not yet owe anyone money. He quickly changed that. Based on a promise by the Théâtre de la Renaissance that they would produce *Das Liebesverbot*, Wagner leased a large house and furnished it comfortably—all on credit. The theater went bankrupt before the opera could be played. Wagner ended up in debtors prison while Minna took in borders. Minna wrote a pleading letter to Wagner's old college friend, Theodore Apel, who sent enough money to bail the composer out of jail.

Their years in Paris, from 1839 to 1842, were filled with frustration and extreme poverty, sometimes leaving them on the edge of starvation. They subsisted on what Wagner could earn copying music for other composers. But Wagner continued to compose passionately, completing *Rienzi* and a year later *The Flying Dutchman*.

Finally, there came a break in fortunes. In October, 1842, *Rienzi* was accepted for performance by the Dresden Opera. It was a grand spectacle in the style of Meyerbeer and a great success. As a result, the Dresden Opera accepted *The Flying Dutchman* and presented it under Wagner's direction in January of 1843. The story of the opera, based on a poem of Heinrich Heine, retells the legend of a man doomed by the Devil to sail the seas until the Day of Judgement—unless he can be redeemed by a woman's fidelity. The theme of redemption through a woman's love appears often in Wagner's opera's. He described the mythical woman as:

> ...*woman in general, though a woman who does not yet exist, one who is longed for and dreamed of, the infinitely womanly woman—let me express it in one phrase: the woman of the future.*

Wagner was appointed Kappelmeister of the opera at a comfortable salary, but the newfound fame and fortune created nearly as many problems as it solved. As news of Wagner's success spread, creditors from all over Europe converged on Dresden, asking for their money. Wagner began another endless round of begging for money from friends, relations and wealthy benefactors. Actually, begging is not the right word, because Wagner was very straightforward in stating that his great talent demanded support. Indulging his genius was the world's responsibility. His creativity required luxurious surroundings, and the stories of Wagner's luxurious lifestyle began circulating around Dresden almost as soon as he set up housekeeping there. By the time he left the city six years later, amounts owed his Dresden creditors alone were more than 13 times his annual salary.

During this period he completed two new operas. *Tannhäuser* was introduced in October of 1845 at Dresden, with his great supporter Schröder-Devrient creating the role of Venus. It was received with hostility by the critics, who considered it pornographic and unmelodic, but it gradually gained popularity with the public. *Lohengrin* was finished three years later, but had not yet been produced. His relationship with the Dresden Opera was rapidly deteriorating and they had continually put off production of the new piece. No one questioned the quality of the music, they were concerned with the growing radical politics of its composer.

Tannhäuser and *Lohengrin* set new standards for German opera, moving beyond the emptiness of French-style Grand Opera. Both stories drew on German mythology and medieval German stories, moving Wagner away from foreign influences and closer to his homeland. The music was powerful and dramatic, intimately involved with the tragic stories instead of being tacked on as an afterthought. But Wagner wanted to institute an even more radical change in opera, a change based largely on his political and social ideas. He wrote a seemingly endless stream of books, essays and newspaper articles to explain his new philosophy. A major new train of thought began with *The Wibelungs*, a confusing mixture of Teutonic poetry, mythology and pseudohistory according to Wagner. The demons of the piece were the French and the Jews. The heroes were the German Volk, whose simple-minded purity Wagner was counting on to rid the world of evil. *The Wibelungs* eventually evolved into an essay titled "The Nibelungen Myth as Scheme for Drama" which contained all the major mythical elements that would become part of *Der Ring des Nibelungen* (*The Ring of the Nibelungen*), the four-opera set that was his life's most remembered work. He was not a very good writer, but there was much beneath his vague, anti-semitic ramblings. In his exploration of classic mythology he was beginning to discover a rich creative vein. The ultimate power of the new musical drama he was developing rested on the ancient foundation of mythology and the power of human archetypes. Wagner however, for the time being, was more interested in writing passionate revolutionary tracts and articles for revolutionary newspapers.

The managers of the Opera were outraged that the King's own employee should be so outspoken about overthrowing the monarchy, and Wagner's professional reputation at Court was in ruins. He was in debt to everyone and had borrowed to the limit from anyone he could buttonhole. He had sold the rights to his existing operas and to operas as yet unwritten. In fact, he often sold the rights to the same opera many times to different people—sometimes even selling the same opera to the same person several times. His relationship with his wife had deteriorated after making no attempt to hide numerous affairs with other women.

When the revolution came, Wagner had very little to lose in Dresden, so he threw himself into the fight with a passion.

There were barricades in the streets. Angry crowds rioted all over Dresden, trying to displace the hated monarch. Bodies were thrown out of fourth story windows. Wagner and Schröder-Devrient and dozens of other idealistic young romantics were caught up in the fever of revolution. The Paris Revolution of 1848 had reached Germany.

While Clara and Robert Schumann, sympathetic to the rebellion but more concerned for the safety of their children, were fleeing for their lives through the darkened fields around Dresden, Wagner took to the streets. He made impassioned political speeches and wrote propaganda pieces for the radical press.

The uprising never really became a revolution, it was merely a riot in the streets which was crushed by Prussian troops within a few days. But Wagner had been identified as a revolutionary and a warrant was issued for his arrest. With Liszt's help and a borrowed passport, he snuck over the border and began wandering around Europe, remaining in exile for 13 years. He could not attend the premiere of *Lohengrin,* which Liszt directed in Weimar on August 28, 1850. Considering Wagner's disgrace, the production was a courageous act. But Liszt's position as grand master of German music set him above politics, and *Lohengrin* became extremely popular. It was performed all over Germany, while Wagner complained that he was the only German who hadn't seen it.

Carl Schurz, the German revolutionary who later emigrated to the U.S. and became a Republican Senator from Missouri, was also in Zurich at this time. He wrote:

> *The most remarkable man I met during this period was Richard Wagner. He had already composed some of his most important works, but his greatness was recognized only by a small circle. He was by no means popular with his fellow-exiles, being regarded as an extremely arrogant and domineering fellow of whom nobody could make a friend, and who treated his wife, a quite attractive, good-natured woman, though not particularly intelligent, in a very unkind manner. If anyone had predicted at that time how remarkable his career would be, nobody would have believed it.*

Lohengrin was finished in 1847, when Wagner was 34. From that year until 1853, when he began composing the score for the *Ring,* he composed nothing. For a man who had always been prolific in his music writing, it was an extraordinary gap. Part of the silence was due to his homelessness and lack of a suitable place to compose. More importantly, however, was his need to reinvent the art form he was trying to master. Traditional German opera simply did not provide him with the scope and potential his vision required. So he set about writing a series of books in which he tried to clarify, for the public and for himself, what his vision of the future of musical drama was. His major works were *The Work of Art of the Future* (1849) and *Opera and Drama* (1850-51). In these books he began to develop an idea of opera that far surpassed anything previously imagined. It was a merging of music, poetry, drama and art that synthesized all types of human creativity, and it would strike at the very heart of human emotions. Some of the emotions were dark and violent, capable of being exploited for evil. Others soared to the highest realms of goodness and virtue, creating a powerful, positive emotional surge. And the responses which Wagner evoked in his friends and in his enemies reflected those two extremes. No other single creative individual in history has ever triggered such a vastly different set of responses in his audiences.

The operas which he had written before were much like older forms. The works that lay ahead, the *Ring*, *Tristan and Isolde*, *Die Meistersinger* and *Parsifal* were the result of his revolutionary new ideas. But they were yet to be written, and Wagner's most pressing immediate need was to find financial and political support for his work. To do this in his years of wandering, he established a pattern of behavior that he repeated again and again.

In 1850, the Laussot family joined together with Wagner's great admirer Frau Julie Ritter of Dresden, to support Wagner with a generous monthly allowance. Visiting Paris, Wagner was a guest in the home of Eugene and Jessie Laussot, a wealthy wine merchant and his 21-year-old English wife. Wagner borrowed money from Laussot, seduced his wife and finally left with hurt feelings when Jessie refused to elope with him. Minna was staying in Dresden. Jessie's husband paid for Wagner's ticket out of town, and astonishingly, his family and Frau Ritter continued to pay Wagner a generous monthly allowance.

The pattern was clear. He showed loyalty to no one except himself and commitment to nothing except his art.

As powerful and world-changing as his art was proven to be, it could never alter the fact that Wagner was a man without ethics or personal honor. He borrowed money without any intention of paying it back and spent it on outrageously extravagant personal indulgences. He made love to any woman he chose, without ever considering the pain it might cause her, his wife or his friends. And he violently lashed out at anyone who criticized or disagreed with him. Other people were simply meant to be used— to support him. He said, "The world owes me what I need," and he said it proudly.

His iron-clad ego protected him from self-doubt, and he continued to create, never questioning the universal importance of his work. His commitment to his art never faltered, and amazingly, the devotion of his many apostles never wavered, even in the face of constant abuse. It's difficult to imagine the strength of personality the man must have had.

In 1853, Wagner had been introduced to Otto and Mathilde Wesendonk, a wealthy silk merchant and his beautiful 28-year-old wife who were convinced of his musical genius. Wesendonk generously built the Wagners a home next to his own villa in Zurich. Wagner accepted large amounts of money from Otto and made love to Mathilde. The bizarre arrangement lasted for almost a year. Otto, aware of the love affair, decided to wait it out. Minna, suffering from a severe heart condition and medicating herself with opium, raged helplessly.

While they were staying with the Wesendoncks, a strange, nervous group gathered for an evening's entertainment. Hans von Bülow and his bride, Cosima, were staying with the Wagners on their honeymoon. Minna, Otto, Hans, Cosima, Mathilde and Wagner all gathered in the parlor to hear Wagner's first reading of *Tristan and Isolde*. Listening to this story of illicit love, betrayal and tragedy, Cosima sat entranced, enchanted by the power of the play. Mathilde collapsed in tears. Minna stomped off in a rage. Hans and Otto sat in impotent silence. Wagner declared the evening a great success and went to bed.

Cosima was shy and withdrawn in the presence of her husband's idol, whom she called "The Great Wagner." She had heard her father's comments about the man's character (or lack of it) and was suspicious of his constant need for money. She was also concerned about the consuming demands he made on Hans and his other followers. Hans would rather work on Wagner's scores and arrangements than on his own work, which displeased her greatly. When she and her new husband left Switzerland, she was relieved to be away from his overpowering presence.

After a series of emotional confrontations with Minna, Wagner tried to convince Mathilde that she should run away with him and abandon her husband. Minna finally put a stop to the affair by begging Otto to keep his wife at home. Their stay had to end. In January of 1859, Otto paid Wagner's way out of town. Watching the sordid resolution of the Wesendonk affair, Cosima and her father were surprisingly understanding. Although they disapproved, they also felt great pity for the man so consumed with passion he could not seem to control his own behavior even when it was ready to destroy him. Liszt wrote the Bülows, "the only way is to accept Wagner as he is, to love him and try to help him as much as possible."

In Berlin, Cosima was doing the same thing for her husband. Bülow was nervous and prone to explosive attacks of temper. His musical talents were great, Liszt and Wagner constantly reassured him of that, but he was susceptible to great self-doubt. The only talent he really believed in was Wagner's. Cosima was more sure of his genius than he was. She secretly commissioned the writing of an opera libretto and gave it to him as a gift, preparing the way for him to begin serious composing. Instead, he set the script aside and went back to work for Wagner, orchestrating the score for *Tristan and Isolde.* Wagner's hold over Bülow grew, and Cosima grew depressed. The death of her brother Daniel in 1859 added to her misery, and when her first daughter, Daniela, was born, she became physically and emotionally ill.

Liszt, too, was having difficult times. His position as chief spokesman and defender of Wagner's "Music of the Future" was making life in Weimar difficult. A great division had grown up between proponents of Wagner's music and defenders of the older, more traditional romantic music pioneered by Schumann and now being carried forward by Johannes Brahms. With Wagner in exile, it was Liszt who had to shoulder the responsibility. And it was at Liszt that the press and the public liked to aim their attacks. In 1860, the Princess left Weimar for Rome, pressing her campaign for an annulment. Liszt was left alone, and he soon grew tired of the empty apartment at Altenberg. He announced his intention to resign his largely honorary position as Kappelmeister in Weimar. In 1861 a great music festival at Weimar celebrated his last appearance—and Wagner's return to Germany. Bülow conducted Liszt's *Faust* Symphony and works by Wagner, and then a large party including Liszt, Bülow, Wagner, Cosima's sister Blandine and her husband all went together to visit Cosima, who was still recovering from her post-baby depression. Seeing Cosima again stirred a strange reaction in Wagner, who told her father, "She is a wild child, but she has great nobility."

After endless battles, Wagner and Minna finally separated. But not before, as a favor to Minna, the German government cancelled the arrest warrant for him and permitted Wagner to live in Germany again. But Wagner was not yet ready to move back into Germany. He traveled around Europe, conducting excerpts from his work, accumulating huge debts and an astonishing wardrobe. In Prague he astonished the natives by appearing in a yellow damask dressing gown, pink tie and a voluminous black velvet cape lined with rose satin. The most embarrassing part of his wardrobe was a pair of kid gloves which he wore as a sign of distaste when forced to conduct Mendelssohn's *Italian Symphony* as part of a concert in London. Wagner had hated the brilliant young conductor since his success in Leipzig, and Wagner's violent jealousy continued even after Mendelssohn's death. So Wagner wore the gloves throughout Mendelssohn's symphony, taking them off only when he proceeded to Weber's *Euryanthe* overture. Those members of the London press who objected to the insult of England's favorite composer he called "a pack of vagabond Jews." His unpleasantness almost cost him a chance to meet with Queen Victoria and Prince Albert. They were devotees of Mendelssohn's work. But they were equally curious about Wagner, who was notorious in England. So they appeared for his last concert. The Queen asked Wagner if any of his operas might be translated into Italian so she could enjoy them.

With Minna safely installed in Dresden, Wagner now settled in the town of Mainz on the Rhine River where the music publisher, Schott, granted him advances for the completion of "a practical operatic comedy suitable to both modest and first-rate theaters." When he wore out his welcome there, he moved on to a stately home in the suburbs of Vienna. He furnished his Viennese bachelor quarters in violet drapes with gold borders, scarlet damask curtains, hangings of silk and velvet on every wall, an incredible profusion of heavy carpets, deep cushions, plush chairs, garlands, flowers and lace. His Viennese seamstress kept a detailed record of every fur-lined pair of satin pants she sewed to match the interior decor, as well as the 24 matching silk dressing gowns. In the cellar were 100 bottles of champagne. He justified it all, again, by saying, "I am a different kind of organism, my nerves are hypersensitive, I must have beauty, splendor and light! The world owes me what I need! I cannot live the miserable life of a town organist, like your Master Bach!" Surrounded by this seemingly essential luxury, he tried to work on the libretto for *Die Meistersinger.*

Even in his palace Wagner was lonely, so he launched an in-depth search for a new female companion. He needed a woman around to make his life completely comfortable. Auditioning a number of possibilities, Wagner for a time kept company with both teenage daughters of the local butcher, as well as several opera singers and actresses. But he now had turned his eye toward a truly major prize—Cosima Liszt von Bülow.

A PASSION FOR OPERA

I am the most German of beings; I am the German spirit. Consider the magic of my works.

—Richard Wagner's Diary

In November of 1863, Wagner stopped in Berlin, planning only to visit with the Bülows between trains. They invited him to dinner at a local hotel and laughed with him while he arranged with a local pawn broker to sell a gold snuff box given to him by an appreciative royal patron. It was worth 270 marks, enough to feed a whole family for months, but just a drop in the bucket compared to the huge sums Wagner now needed to settle his debts. Hans was to conduct that night, and he convinced Wagner to stay over and hear the performance. Looking into the face of the woman he now so deeply wanted, Wagner agreed. Hans left dinner early to prepare for the concert, while Wagner and Cosima lingered over dinner, talking and eventually making confessions. The attraction was mutual. In the horsedrawn coach on the way to the performance, Wagner remembered their final surrender:

> *We gazed speechless into each other's eyes; an intense longing for an avowal of the truth mastered us and led to a confession— which needed no words—of the boundless unhappiness which oppressed us.*

With tears and kisses, they sealed their vows to belong to each other.

Cosima was mesmerized with Wagner, worshiping his genius and obsessed by his overwhelming personality. She was also growing increasingly disappointed with her husband, whose talents were not reaching her expectation. Wagner was a man whose powers matched those of her own great father. They began a passionate romance, but kept it a deep secret.

Cosima was happy to avoid a confrontation. She was not prepared to leave her home and her children, and Wagner was in no position to support anyone, even himself. He faced total and complete financial ruin. Borrowing at exorbitant interest rates to pay old bills, he was buried under pyramiding debt. Begging letters went out, but he had gone to the well once too often. No one would give him anything.

In Vienna, the creditors were closing in and the only possibility seemed another term in debtors prison. But still his spirits were irrepressible. His companion, Wendelin Weissheimer, remembered this typical episode in his memoirs:

> *Wagner had been staying at his hotel for two months. He was still hoping for the payment which was to be made to him after the first performance of Tristan, but it did not arrive— the proprietor became worried and sent him one bill after the other... When one evening I went to visit him, he was full of woe and bemoaned his miserable position. Full of sympathy we listened to him and sat down on the sofa in deep depression, while he was pacing up and down in nervous haste. Suddenly he stopped dead and said: "Ah, now I know what is missing and what*

I need." He ran to the door and rang the bell loudly. The waiter finally appeared, slowly and with hesitation, for these people soon know which way the wind is blowing, and he was no less amazed than we were when Wagner ordered: "Will you bring us immediately two bottles of champagne on ice!...For God's sake, in this situation!" we cried out when the waiter had left again. But he gave us a fervent lecture on the absolute necessity of champagne especially in desperate situations—only champagne could help one to overcome such embarrassments...If you associated with Wagner you went from surprise to surprise. When I entered his room next morning he showed me 1000 guilder which the Empress had sent him.

Once again, Wagner left town and went to Switzerland. He traveled by way of Munich, which was draped in black to mourn the death of King Maximillian. Walking past a shop window, Wagner saw the portrait of a beautiful, effeminate young man, the newest King Ludwig.

In Switzerland, he asked Otto Wesendonk for his old house back. Otto and Mathilde, who were happily reunited and enjoying their new baby, had no intention of letting Wagner back into their lives. Otto offered him a little money if he promised to stay out of town. Wagner continued on to Stuttgart to his friend Karl Eckert. Wagner was exhausted and bitter, telling a friend "only a miracle can save me now." While he sat in Eckert's parlor, a mysterious man appeared at the door asking for Wagner. His card said he was Herr Pfistermeister, "Secretary to the King of Bavaria." Sure that this was just a clever plot by his creditors to smoke him out of hiding, Wagner sent the maid out with a message that Herr Wagner was not there.

When he returned to his hotel, there was another message. It was urgent that the King's Secretary meet with Wagner. The next morning, Herr Pfistermeister arrived and ceremoniously handed to Wagner the King's signet ring and photo, inscribed with a message of almost embarrassing affection.

The King had been in love with Wagner's music since he was a small boy. Now he was in love with Wagner. In Wagner's operas, he found "heavenly joy amid earthly pain." He wanted to pay off all the debts, give Wagner a generous allowance and build him a house next door to the castle where he could compose in peace. It was a miracle worthy of its own opera.

His pockets filled with large amounts of the King's money, Wagner went back to Vienna and tried to buy back his belongings that had been auctioned off. In a display of selfishness remarkable even for Wagner, he paid only the most pressing commercial bills and did not repay any of the old and dear friends who had supported him for years. Claiming the King has given him only a "small salary," he abandoned them and pocketed the remainder of the money.

Wagner took up residence in the Imperial Capital of Munich at the Villa Pellet. His very first thought was to send for Hans von Bülow. Desperate for some company besides the obsessive young king, Wagner wrote to Berlin and asked Hans to bring his wife and family down to Munich for the summer. The couple now had another daughter, Blandine. Hans could not resist Wagner, and Cosima too was unable to hold back any longer. Her passionate nature had found a home at last. Although she loved her husband, it was really a friendship based on affection mixed with pity. It was not the love of which she knew she was capable. She was destined for a greater mission; something that would challenge her abilities, her talents and her heart. Cosima was in search of a relationship more important than anything else.

On June 29, 1864, Cosima and her children arrived in Munich to join Wagner. Her husband would follow a week later. But in that short, passionate week, the die was cast. Richard and Cosima's daughter Isolde was conceived. When Hans arrived, the three of them settled in together for a painful summer.

Wagner had arranged for the King to offer Bülow an excellent job as Court Pianist. It would assure Wagner that his greatest musical assistant would be nearby, and it would provide a perfect excuse for Cosima to move permanently to Munich from Berlin. It was a difficult decision for Hans to make. Accepting the position in Munich would mean putting his fate completely in Wagner's hands—and giving up his own dream as a composer. Life around Wagner precluded having creative ideas of one's own. But his commitment to Wagner had long since become complete, and he accepted the position. Cosima set up housekeeping for them in Munich and immediately began dividing her time between her small house and Wagner's grand new estate. She was Wagner's hostess, secretary and confidant. Her husband did not yet know she was also his lover.

As usual, Wagner was doing his best to make a hash of things. Given an almost bottomless source of funds, he indulged in an orgy of lavish spending. This immediately made enemies for him among the King's financial advisors. To make matters worse, he began advising the young King on political matters, a tactic guaranteed to earn him more enemies at court. Local musicians of Munich bitterly resented his high-handed tactics. Amazingly enough, he even managed to offend the King, who totally worshiped him. Being addressed with condescending familiarity that broke all rules of protocol made the King very uncomfortable. Even worse, news of Wagner's affair with Cosima got back to the King and caused him to become extremely jealous.

The only person who could smooth things over was Cosima, who began to handle all contact between the court and Wagner. She became a good friend and confidant of the King and protected Wagner's interests whenever she could. Fortunately, the King's ultimate obsession was Wagner's work, and *Tristan and Isolde* held more than enough wild passion to satisfy the royal patron. Hans von Bülow began preparing its production with the Munich Opera company. A newspaper article described a typical rehearsal:

> *Bülow raps with his baton: "Gentlemen, if you please, let us begin." he calls in his thin, hoarse voice to the orchestra, which has been augmented by various brass players and numbers ninety. The music begins, Bülow uses his whole body to indicate the nuances he wants and puts such ferocious energy into each gesture that one begins to tremble for the violinists and the lamps within his reach.*
>
> *The other man who arrived with Bülow stands on the stage. It is Richard Wagner, with the bird-like features that all Germany knows. In a state of continuous excitement that makes one nervous, he accompanies every note sung with a corresponding gesture that the singers imitate as closely as they can; only someone who has seen the composer toiling and gesticulating in this way can have any idea of the multitude of nuances that he wants to be conveyed. Almost every step, every movement of a hand, every opening door, is 'musically illustrated,' and*

there is in Die Meistersinger, *in particular, such a quantity of music illustrative of the singers' mime that we would regard it as miraculous if a production of the opera that was not rehearsed under the composer's supervision managed to introduce all the actions intended to accompany this music. Only when Fräulein Mallinger is singing does Wagner suspend his instructions, listens with visible pleasure, trots to and fro with one hand in his trouser pocket, sits down on a chair beside the prompter's box, gives pleased, approving nods and smiles all over his face. But if something in the orchestral playing displeases him, which happens rather often, he leaps up as if bitten by a snake, clapping his hands, Bülow stops and raps his baton and Wagner calls to the players: "Piano, gentlemen, piano! That must be soft, soft, soft, as if it's coming to us from another world." And the orchestra starts again. "More piano!" Wagner shouts, and makes the appropriate gesture with his hands. "So, so, so—good, good, good-beautiful." And so it goes on like that all evening.*

It was during a rehearsal of *Tristan* on the morning of April 12 that Cosima gave birth to her third—and Wagner's first—child, Isolde. Still maintaining the myth of her marriage to Hans, she continued to run two households, act as intermediary between Wagner and Ludwig's ministers and added the role of biographer to her duties. Ludwig asked her to write Wagner's life story, based on the Master's dictation. The result is *Mein Leben,* Wagner's occasionally factual autobiography.

By 1865, her position as Wagner's constant companion was obvious to everyone in Munich. Even Hans, who so desperately wanted to save his wife's honor and his own dignity, could not ignore it. And the mounting pressure to rein in his wild composer was becoming impossible for Ludwig to resist. He asked Wagner to quietly leave town. Before dawn on a cold December morning, Wagner boarded a train for Switzerland, accompanied only by his faithful old dog, Pohl. Traveling first to Zurich and then to the south of France, Wagner had a sad trip. In Marseille, his dog died and within a week, he received word that his wife Minna had also died after a long battle with heart disease.

Back in Munich, it was up to Cosima and Hans to hold out in the "enemy camp." Hans continued defending the music and Cosima kept relations calm with the King. Finally, both Cosima and Wagner were so depressed by their separation that they decided to meet in Geneva for a month. Since the beginning of the year, her husband had increasingly become aware of their intimacy. He was willing to ignore the affair and hope it would pass as long as she was discreet, but it was essential to keep up appearances. Her trip to Geneva, however, made the liaison impossible to ignore. The newspapers, already critical of Wagner, now had more ammunition with which to criticize him. But it was vital to put the rumors to rest. All their livelihoods depended on the King and his favor, so the three decided to put on a solid front. Wagner's new home, "Triebschen," was remote and secluded, nestled on the shores of Switzerland's lake Lucerne. To this refuge they retreated: Hans, Cosima, Richard and all the children. Throughout the summer of 1866 they lived together, trapped in a hell of their own creation. They managed to appease the King, but it made them all physically and emotionally ill. In February of the next year, Richard and Cosima's second daughter, Eva, was born. Hans was on the verge of a nervous breakdown, but the facade still had to be maintained.

With the King pacified, banishment was lifted. Hans and Cosima moved back to Munich, where Wagner had convinced the King to appoint Bülow head of the new music school and director of the opera. The Bülows moved into a large apartment together and to all appearances the affair was over. *Lohengrin* and *Tannhäuser* were both in production, conducted by Bülow, and nothing could be allowed to interfere with the work. Wagner remained alone at Triebschen, miserable without Cosima, attempting to complete the score for *Die Meistersinger von Nürnberg (The Mastersinger of Nuremberg)*. All three were abjectly unhappy, but they were trapped by their own ambition, afraid that revealing the truth would end King Ludwig's support.

Liszt fought passionately against a divorce. He had recently taken minor orders in the Catholic church and the idea of divorce upset him terribly. But even more importantly, Liszt felt great compassion for Bülow, whom he still thought of as a devoted pupil and valued friend. A divorce would, in one blow, take away Bülow's family, wife, best friend and life's work. It seemed like too great a price to pay. But in June of 1869, Wagner's third child and first son, Siegfried, was born, and the secret could no longer be maintained. Leaving her oldest two daughters with their grandmother, Cosima took Wagner's children and openly joined him at Triebschen. That day, she began a diary which would record the story of her life with Wagner for their children. It began:

> *In order that you may understand, I must confess to you that up to the hour in which I recognized my true inner calling, my life had been a dreary, unbeautiful dream, of which I have no desire to tell you anything, for I do not understand it myself and reject it with the whole of my now purified soul. The outward appear-*

*ance was and remained calm, but inside all was
bleak and dreary, when there came into my life
that being who swiftly led me to realize that up
to now I had never lived. My love became for me
a rebirth, a deliverance, a fading away of all
that was trivial and bad in me, and I swore to
seal it through death, through pious renuncia-
tion or complete devotion. What love has done
for me I shall never be able to repay.*

In a letter to Cosima's sister, Bülow shared his agony:

*Believe me, I have done everything
humanly possible to avoid a public scandal. For
more than three years I have lived a life of
indescribable torment. You simply cannot imagine the consuming agitations to which I was
continuously subjected. In the end I sacrificed
my whole artistic and material existence. The
only thing left to sacrifice was my life—that, I
must confess, would have been the simplest
method of solving the problem, of cutting this
complex knot. This sacrifice I was not prepared
to make—can anyone blame me? But perhaps I
would even have taken this course of action if,
on the part of that other one who is as sublime in
his works as he is unspeakably low in his deeds,
I had discovered the least trace of honor, just one
expression of some basic feeling of decency...*

  *It was only a few months ago that, through
the press, I came to know of the Master's good
fortune that his mistress (whose name was given
in full) had at long last presented him with a son
who was to be christened Siegfried as a good
omen for the completion of his new opera. I have
thus been crowned most magnificently with the*

*horns of a cuckold. Unfortunately I could not
flee from Munich—but the tortures of hell which
I have had to suffer there during the last months
of my activity cannot be imagined...I only had
the choice of two alternatives: either be treated
with degrading pity as an individual who had
no idea of things which were common knowledge, or else be considered so infamous as to be
the protégé of the royal protégé at such a price.*

Hans von Bülow left Munich in agony. The King
sulked in one of his Bavarian fantasy castles. Liszt
withdrew to a cloister outside Rome. Cosima, although
certain of the rightness of her decision, suffered terrible
guilt and remorse over her treatment of Hans. Only
Wagner was happy, finally able to live peacefully at
Triebschen with all five of the children. Cosima filed for
a divorce, which was granted in July of 1870. She was 34
and Wagner was 65. The next month they were married,
and in her diary Cosima said:

*My prayers have been concentrated upon
two points: Richard's well-being and my hope
that I may always be able to promote it, and
Hans' happiness and my hope that he may live a
cheerful life—far from me.*

Wagner, whose relationship with the King was
growing more distant, began looking for a new musical
home. He was no longer interested in Munich, where his
influence was now strongly resisted. His dream was to
build a great new theater, designed specifically to produce his plays and dedicated only to their performance.
To do this, he would need a new patron, and the year 1871
seemed to offer one. In January, Kaiser Wilhelm I
proclaimed the Second German Reich and was victorious

over the French in the Franco-Prussian war. Embarrassingly willing to abandon his long-time protector Ludwig, Wagner instantly shifted allegiance to the Prussian dictator and began courting his favor.

Wagner's sudden political shifts may be a little difficult to understand, considering how passionately he defended his beliefs at the time he adopted them. His instant political swings from revolutionary to royalist or from royalist to militarist are often explained as a simple matter of economics. But they also result from Wagner's constantly changing posture as the ultimate political romantic. Romanticism is a world of emotional extremes. Politically, romantics often gravitate to the far left or the far right—becoming passionate anarchists or devout fascists. Revolution and autocracy are the ultimate extremes of romanticism. The calm moderation of the Republic, with its need for reason and compromise, doesn't appeal to the extreme romantic. Wagner played both sides of the field, first as a fire-breathing revolutionary in 1849, then as a devoted subject of King Ludwig in Munich, and finally as a militaristic believer in Kaiser Wilhelm's "Teutomania."

Given the ability to adapt his beliefs to the times, it is no surprise that the *third* German Reich also found it convenient to adapt Wagner's music and ideas to their own ends. The same vein of radical German romanticism was the source of their power.

In 1869, King Ludwig finally grew tired of waiting for Wagner and demanded that an opera—any opera—be produced in Munich. He had spent millions because he loved Wagner's work so much, and now he longed to hear it. Wagner refused. Having abandoned Munich, he did not want anything performed there. He was determined to find a new location for his productions. But the King insisted and *Das Rhinegold*, the first opera of the four-play

Ring cycle, was performed in Munich. Wagner boycotted the production and refused to let anyone he knew conduct or sing in the performance. The next year, *Die Walküre*, second play of the *Ring* cycle, was performed in Munich, again at the King's insistence. Wagner again boycotted.

In 1871, Wagner chose the little town of Bayreuth as the site for his new opera house and set about finding the money to build it. For the next four years, he and Cosima crisscrossed Europe, raising money for the new festival, which would feature a complete production of all four *Ring* operas, performed on four consecutive nights. Ironically, the Kaiser in whom he had placed so much hope, had no interest in providing any help at all. Once again, Wagner's savior was King Ludwig who loaned the festival 100,000 Thalers and continued to pay Wagner a generous allowance. The final scores of *Siegfried* and *Götterdämmerung*, the last two plays of the cycle, were completed in November of 1874 and rehearsals began in the summer of 1875. Finally, after years of struggle, the first Bayreuth Festival was presented in August of 1876.

It was an artistic success and a financial failure, leaving behind a huge debt. Instead of preparing to produce the next year's festival, Wagner and Cosima were now faced with a six-year-long struggle to put the festival on sound financial footing. During those years, while playing concerts all across Europe to raise funds, Wagner found time to create his final opera, *Parsifal.* It was produced at the second Bayreuth festival in July of 1882 when Wagner was 69.

In 1883, suffering from serious heart disease, Wagner traveled with his family to Venice, where he sought warmer weather and a peace that was not possible in the excitement of the festival city. In Venice, at the age of 70, he died of a heart attack. Cosima clung to his body for 25 hours after his death. Finally, taking a scissors from his desk, she cut off the long, silver-blond hair that he loved and placed it on his chest in the coffin. The Italian doctor who wrote Wagner's death certificate said, "I do not know who these people are, but never have I seen a wife so consumed by her husband."

Three weeks after Wagner's death, a small and solemn group met in the Bayreuth theater. Conductor Adolf von Gross read a letter from Wagner containing instructions for performance of *Parsifal.* Cosima remained absolutely silent, hidden behind a black veil. Wagner left no will, and the question of who would succeed him as director at Bayreuth was unanswered. The group, with unspoken agreement from Cosima, decided to produce only *Parsifal* that year, under Gross's direction, but named no permanent festival director.

Lost in her grief, Cosima returned to Wahnfried and spent her days sitting next to Wagner's tomb, seeing no one and speaking only to her children.

Gradually, Cosima began to emerge. The powerful force that pulled her out of seclusion was her dedication to the memory of Richard Wagner. In life, her devotion to him had been total. Now, she promoted his work with the single-minded passion of a religious zealot. In the festival theater she ordered the carpenters to build a special hidden box giving her full view of stage and orchestra. Invisible behind her screen, she passed notes to the orchestra director, the singers and the stage managers. In her encyclopedic mind was a perfectly preserved memory of each detail of the Master's stage direction, and she was determined to preserve a performance style that exactly matched his vision. Cosima had studied the art of total self-discipline and emotional control from her Russian governess; she had studied the power of controlling others from the master, Herr Wagner. Now, she put those lessons to work. Fighting off attacks from many others who wanted to take over the reigns in Bayreuth, she established herself as the complete master over artistic direction and financial administration. By 1886, three years after Wagner's death, she was officially in charge of the whole Bayreuth organization.

During that three-year period, Cosima never saw her father. Liszt had traveled to Bayreuth to see a *Parsifal* performance in 1884, but Cosima refused to see him. There is no record of any argument between them and Liszt was mystified by his daughter's coldness. Finally, in the spring of 1886, she broke her silence and traveled to Weimar to visit the old man.

Liszt was 74. His once trim figure had grown heavy and stooped, his eyes a little dim and his great head of hair completely grey. But his enthusiasm for performance and composition were undiminished. In the last few months, admirers in Paris, London, St. Petersburg, Budapest and Weimar hosted anniversary performances of his music—and Liszt attended them all. His popularity in London was remarkable, rivaling the excitement he had created 62 years before as a child prodigy. The Queen invited him to Windsor palace for a private performance and remarked that Liszt, "having been a very wild, phantastic looking man, was now a quiet benevolent-looking old priest, with long white hair and scarcely any teeth."

Cosima invited her father to his granddaughter, Daniela's, wedding in July. He happily accepted the offer and joined the party in Bayreuth on July 2. After traveling to Luxembourg for a final concert performance at the casino on July 19, Liszt returned to Bayreuth to attend performances of *Parsifal* and *Tristan*. He caught a severe cold on the train, and sat huddled in the Wagner family box, covering his wracking coughs with a handkerchief.

On the the 31st of July, 1886, Liszt died of pneumonia, lying alone in a boarding house near the theater. Cosima, who had not offered him a room at Wahnfried—even during his illness—refused to allow him the last rights of the Catholic church and ordered that he be buried in Bayreuth, instead of in Rome as he had asked. No performances were cancelled at the theater, but hundreds of students from across Europe gathered in Bayreuth to honor their teacher. They followed his casket to the cemetery in a noisy, not-very-solemn crowd and gathered around pianos throughout the city to play Liszt's music and celebrate his life.

In the next decade, Cosima made certain that Bayreuth and the festival became the world capital of Wagner worship. The "perfect Wagnerites," as George Bernard Shaw called them, were drawn to this small German village as if on pilgrimage. Wagner's music and his philosophy spread rapidly away from Bayreuth, taking the world by storm.

The first cultural center to come under Wagnerian domination was Paris in the late 1880s. Writers, painters and philosophers all began to discuss their work from a Wagnerian point of view. The French composer, Debussy, was haunted by his work, and the painters Cézanne, Gauguin and Renoir were all impressed with his thought. Next to fall under his influence was London. Shaw wrote a socialist interpretation of Wagner's operas, T.S. Eliot quoted Wagner in *The Wasteland* and James Joyce evoked Wagnerian images in *Ulysses*. *The Work of*

Art of the Future seemed to be just that, with Wagner societies springing up around the world.

Cosima reigned over the entire festival, fiercely preserving the memory of her husband and his ideals. Under her leadership, the programs acquired their permanent character; each year *Parsifal*, the *Ring* and one additional opera were performed. The festival became an established event and an international drawing card for both intellectuals and social climbers.

Hans von Bülow, finally free of Wagner's influence, was able to break away from Bayreuth and establish a successful career of his own. As the conductor of the Meiningen orchestra, he was an outspoken promoter of Johannes Brahms, and gained a reputation for biting wit in music criticism. Bülow married the actress Marie Schanzer in 1882 and died while on vacation in Cairo, Egypt in 1894.

In 1906, Cosima suffered a physical collapse and handed over management of the festival to her son, Siegfried. He continued her conservative-style management of the festival while she went into retirement. For the next 23 years, she was an invalid who gradually lost touch with reality. The last ten years of Cosima's life were a vague, disoriented time in which she slipped back and forth between the present and the past. On her ninetieth birthday, when her children told her how old she was, she laughed and said, "Am I really?" She died in 1930 at the age of 93.

A CONTEMPORARY CHRONOLOGY

1770   12/17   Ludwig van Beethoven is baptized in Bonn, Germany.

1781   The Leipzig town council votes to build a public concert hall called the Gewandhaus.

1785   8/18   Friedrich Wieck is born in a hamlet on the Elbe River.

1791   12/5   Wolfgang Amadeus Mozart dies in Vienna.

1795   Beethoven makes his public debut as pianist and composer.

1806   10/14   Napoleon defeats the Prussians at Jena, 40 miles northwest of Zwickau.

1809   2/3   Felix Mendelssohn is born in Hamburg. He is the son of Abraham and Leah Mendelssohn and the grandson of Moses Mendelssohn, noted 18th century philosopher.

                Birthdays of Abraham Lincoln, Charles Darwin, Edgar Allen Poe, Oliver Wendell Holmes.

1810   3/1   Fryderyk Chopin is born in Zelazowa Wol, near Warsaw, Poland.

        6/8   Robert Schumann is born in Zwickau, Saxony.

1811   10/22   Franz (Ferencz) Liszt is born in Raiding (Doborján), western Hungary.

1812   Napoleon marches through Zwickau with 150,000 French soldiers on his way to conquer Russia. A two-year-old Robert Schumann watches in awe.

1813   5/21   Napoleon loses the pivotal Battle of Leipzig.

        5/22   Richard Wagner is born in Leipzig.

        10/10   Giuseppe Verdi is born in Le Roncole, Italy. He will become the 19th century's greatest Italian opera composer.

1814   Friedrich Wieck begins accepting piano students in Leipzig.

1816   Friedrich Wieck marries 19-year-old Marianne Tromlitz.

1817   Carl Maria von Weber is appointed by the King of Saxony to organize the performance of German opera at Dresden.

1818   9/13   Clara Josephine Wieck is born in Leipzig.

1820   Liszt, the child prodigy, performs a subscription concert at Eszterházy palace to raise funds for his own education.

1821   5/5   Napoleon dies in exile.

        6/18   Weber's *Der Freischütz*, the first German romantic opera, receives an exceptional response at its premiere.

                The Mendelssohn family converts to Christianity in order to avoid discrimination.

                Felix Mendelssohn performs with Carl Maria von Weber.

Liszt studies with Czerny in Vienna.

Wagner is orphaned for a second time with the death of his step-father Ludwig Geyer.

1823   Clara Wieck's parents divorce, her mother loses custody and Clara is sent to live with Friedrich Wieck.

Liszt receives the blessing of Ludwig van Beethoven.

1824 9/14   Clara Wieck's training begins on the day after her fifth birthday.

5/7   Beethoven's Ninth Symphony premieres in Vienna.

Liszt first visits England.

1826   Schumann's sister commits suicide and his father dies.

Mendelssohn, age 17, writes *A Midsummer Night's Dream Overture*.

6/5   Carl Maria von Weber dies in London.

1827   The Wagner family moves to Leipzig.

1828 3/31   Robert Schumann, an 18-year-old Leipzig University law student, meets his future piano teacher, Friedrich Wieck, and his future wife, Clara Wieck, at a musical evening in the home of friends.

1829 8/11   Chopin performs his first highly successful concert in Vienna.

10/20 Clara Wieck makes her first public appearance, playing a duet at the Gewandhaus.

1829   10/22   Nicolo Paganini, the great violin virtuoso, performs in Leipzig. After hearing Clara Wieck, he is enchanted with her musical talents.

Schumann ends his piano lessons with Friedrich Wieck and goes to Heidelberg to study law for a year.

1830   Easter   Schumann hears Paganini perform in Heidelberg and writes a letter to his mother, pleading with her to let him study music.

8/21   Friedrich Wieck offers to take Schumann back as a pupil and train him to be a piano virtuoso. Schumann's mother relents and he gives up law school.

10/30   Schumann returns to Leipzig and moves into the Wieck home.

11/8   Clara Wieck's first solo performance at the Gewandhaus.

12/25   Wagner's composition, Overture in B flat, is performed in a Leipzig Christmas concert. It is the subject of laughter and derision.

12   Liszt introduces himself to Hector Berlioz and hears the first performance of Berlioz's *Symphonie Fantastique.*

1831   1/11   Schumann completes his first composition, *Variations On A Theme ABEGG.* He plays them for Wagner, who responds, "I hate them."

Schumann and the Wieck family discover Chopin's *Variations On A Theme by Mozart.* Schumann publishes his famous magazine review of Chopin, "Hats off, Gentlemen, a genius."

9/30   Clara and Friedrich Wieck leave Leipzig on Clara's first concert tour.

Chopin arrives in Paris.

1832   2/26   Chopin's premier performance in Paris receives poor public acceptance, but greatly impresses Mendelssohn, Liszt and opera composer Giacomo Meyerbeer. Upon hearing of Warsaw's capture by the Russians, he writes his *Etude* in C minor, the *Revolutionary Etude*.

3/22   Johann Wolfgang von Goethe dies. The poetry of this great German writer inspired music by Mendelssohn, Schumann, Berlioz, Liszt, Beethoven and Schubert.

1833   Schumann and his friends begin the *New Journal for Music (Die Neue Zeitschrift für Musik)*.

Wagner is named Kapellmeister (chorusmaster) of the Würzburger Theater and writes his first complete opera, *Die Feen (The Fairies)* which is not produced until five years after his death.

Liszt meets Countess Marie d'Agoult at the home of Marquise de Vayer.

5/7   Johannes Brahms is born in a tenement on the waterfront of Hamburg, Germany.

1834   Ernestine von Fricken, daughter of Baron von Fricken, comes to study with Friedrich Wieck.

Wagner is appointed conductor of the Magdeburg Opera.

1835   Mendelssohn is named musical director of Leipzig Gewandhaus Orchestra.

     9/13   Clara Wieck's birthday party is attended by Felix Mendelssohn and Robert Schumann.

Liszt and Marie d'Agoult run away together to Switzerland.

12/18   Liszt and Marie d'Agoult's child, Blandine, is born.

1836   3/29   The premier of Wagner's opera *Das Liebesverbot* is a total fiasco. The second performance opens to an empty house and the Magdeburg opera company dissolves into bankruptcy.

Wagner is named conductor of Königsberg theater. The theater closes immediately after Wagner assumes the job.

Schumann's mother dies.

11/24   Wagner marries actress Minna Planer in Königsberg.

1837   Queen Victoria ascends the throne of England.

Wagner is named conductor of Riga, Russia opera.

Liszt wins piano duel with Thalberg in Paris.

12/26   Liszt and Marie d'Agoult's daughter, Cosima, is born in Lake Como, Italy.

1838	Chopin falls ill.
1839	Wagner flees Russia under cover of darkness.
5/9	Liszt and Countess d'Agoult's son, Daniel Liszt, is born in Rome, Italy.
1840	Wagner's *Das Liebesverbot* is accepted for performance at Théâtre de la Renaissance but the opera company goes broke before it can be performed. Wagner is imprisoned twice for debts.
	Liszt meets Robert Schumann in Leipzig.
	Liszt meets Richard Wagner in Paris.
8/12	The Saxon court grants Robert Schumann and Clara Wieck permission to marry without her father's consent.
9/12	Robert and Clara are married in Schönfeld on the day before her twenty-first birthday.
	Liszt performs in England, Scotland and Ireland.
	Liszt performs in Belgium, Germany and Denmark.
	Liszt performs in Weimar, Dresden and Leipzig.
1842 10/20	Wagner's opera, *Rienzi*, receives great popular success in its premier at the Dresden Opera. Wagner's name immediately becomes known throughout Germany.
	Mendelssohn makes command performances at Buckingham Palace for Queen Victoria.

Liszt performs in Russia.

1843 1/2 Wagner's opera, *Die fliegende Holländer (The Flying Dutchman)*, is presented under his direction by the Dresden Opera.

2 Wagner is appointed musical director of the Dresden Opera.

4/3 Mendelssohn founds the Leipzig Conservatory and hires Robert Schumann to teach classes in piano and composition.

9/1 Liszt is appointed Kapellmeister of Weimar.

Giacomo Meyerbeer, a German Jew with an Italian name and the undisputed master of the grand opera, is named Kapellmeister to the King of Prussia in Berlin.

1844 Liszt formally separates from the Countess d'Agoult.

1847 2 The first performances of Wagner's *Tannhäuser* and Schumann's *Faust* take place under the direction of Liszt at Weimar.

11/4 Mendelssohn dies of a stroke.

Liszt meets Princess Carolyne Sayne-Wittgenstein in Kiev.

1848 2/16 Chopin gives his last public appearance, a concert in Paris.

Wagner's *Lohengrin* is turned down by the Dresden Opera.

Wagner joins revolutionaries in Saxony. After the revolution aborts, Wagner leaves for Switzerland under threat of arrest.

1849   2/16   Liszt produces *Tannhäuser* at Weimar. Wagner is unable to attend because of outstanding warrants.

       10/17 Chopin dies in Paris. At his request, Mozart's *Requiem* is sung at his funeral.

1850   8/26   *Lohengrin* premieres at Weimar under Liszt's direction.

              Violinist Joseph Joachim is chosen to lead the Weimar orchestra.

              Wagner anonymously publishes "On Judaism in Music" in the *Neue Zeitshrift,* which is no longer under Schumann's editorial direction.

1851   Hans von Bülow becomes Liszt's pupil.

1852   Wagner completes the text of the four opera cycle *Der Ring des Nibelungen (The Ring of the Nibelungs).* Completing the work will take the next 25 years.

1853   Brahms meets Hungarian violinist Remény and begins a European tour as Remény's accompanist.

              Verdi's *Il Trovatore* and *La Traviata* premier.

              Brahms meets Joseph Joachim, who will become his best friend and first important promoter.

       6   Brahms and Remény make an unsuccessful visit to Liszt at Altenburg. Remény dismisses Brahms and leaves him to find his own way across Germany on foot.

9/30 On the advice of Joachim, Brahms introduces himself to Robert and Clara Schumann at Düseldorf. They become his ardent supporters and invite him to visit them for the next month.

10/28 Schumann publishes an enthusiastic article about Brahms in the *New Journal,* arranges for his music to be published and sets up a performance for Brahms in Leipzig.

7 Liszt goes to Zurich to visit Wagner.

10 Wagner is joined by Bülow, Liszt, Joachim, Remény and Richard Pohl in Switzerland.

1855 Princess Carolyne's husband obtains a civil divorce.

1856 7/29 Robert Schumann dies in Düsseldorf.

Liszt and Princess Carolyne visit Wagner in Zurich.

1857 8/18 Bülow marries Cosima Liszt in Berlin.

The Wagners settle into a home built for them next door to Otto and Mathilde Wesendonck. Wagner stops work on everything else and writes *Tristan and Isolde* under Mathilde's inspiration.

1859 Liszt quarrels with Wagner about the situation with Mathilde Wesendonck but continues to promote his work.

12/13 Daniel Liszt, Cosima's brother, dies in Berlin.

1860 3 The Brahms-Joachim "Manifesto against the Music of the Future" is published in *Das Echo.*

	5	Princess Carolyne goes to Rome to obtain a divorce.
1861	8	"Music of the Future" club meets at Weimar—Wagner, Bülow and Liszt attend.
	10	Liszt's marriage to Princess Carolyne is cancelled at the last moment.
1862	9/8	Brahms leaves Hamburg for Vienna, where he establishes his permanent home.
1864		Meyerbeer dies.
	3/10	King Ludwig I, a youthful fan of Wagner, ascends the Bavarian throne.
	3/10	Wagner flees his creditors (again).
	5/3	King Ludwig sends for Wagner, pays all his debts and moves him into a home next door to the palace.
1865		Liszt receives the religious title of Abbé in Rome, but doesn't exactly lead a life of poverty, chastity and obedience.

A daughter, Isolde, is born to Wagner and Cosima von Bülow, who are both still married to other people. Scandal rocks Munich and the King is disturbed.

Threatened by political and personal scandals, Ludwig asks Wagner to leave Munich, but continues his allowance.

1866	1/25	Minna Wagner dies. Cosima von Bülow, still married to Hans, settles in Lucerne, Switzerland with Wagner.
1868		The first performance of *Die Meistersinger*

is presented under the baton of Hans von Bülow, who is broken-hearted but still a supporter of Wagner.

The philosopher, Friedrich Nietzche, becomes a disciple of Wagner and secretly falls in love with Cosima. He lives with them at their home, Triebshen, in Lucerne.

1869   2/18   First complete performance of Brahms' *A German Requiem*, composed in part to commemorate his mother and Robert Schumann, is a triumphant success in Leipzig.

Wagner publishes a new version of "Judaism in Music" under his own name and with a new appendix.

Das Rheingold is first performed in Munich at King Ludwig's order. Wagner boycotts the performance.

1870   6/26   *Die Walkure* premieres in Munich, again at the King's insistence. Wagner again boycotts.

1871   Wagner switches political allegiance from King Ludwig, who is no longer a major power in Germany, to the Prussian Kaiser. The King continues paying him an allowance.

1872   Wagner, Cosima and their children settle in the German city of Bayreuth.

5/22   The foundation stone is laid for the new Wagnerian theater in Bayreuth.

9   Brahms is named artistic director of the *Gesellschaft Der Musikfreunde*.

1876		The first performance of the *Ring* cycle at Bayreuth takes place.
1882		The first performance of *Parsifal* at Bayreuth takes place.
1883	2/13	Wagner dies in Venice.
1886	7/31	Liszt dies in Bayreuth.
1896	5/20	Clara Schumann dies in Frankfurt.
1897	4/3	Brahms dies in Vienna.
1930	4/1	Cosima Liszt von Bülow Wagner dies in Bayreuth.

LISTENING TO THE ROMANTICS

Novice classical music collectors may have trouble knowing where to start. The huge number of available recordings can be intimidating. As seasoned veterans, we begin to discover the selection isn't as wide as we once thought. There are a great many recordings of a few standard pieces of repertoire, and beyond that, the options become more limited.

These recommendations are designed to help with both problems. For the newcomer to classical music, we've recommended some good compact disk versions of the basic library—to cut through the fog. In addition, we've included some more unusual selections now available on compact disk—to widen the horizons.

This is not a comprehensive discography. For that, you should consult Schwann's quarterly publication, *Opus,* available at most music stores. It catalogs every classical recording currently in print and makes a wonderful wish list.

ROBERT SCHUMANN
During each phase of his life, Robert Schumann wrote a different type of music. He began with miniatures—little piano pieces filled with power and passion. Then he moved on to songs and chamber music that opened his heart and broadened his musical horizons. By the end of his life, Schumann had created four major symphonies, an opera and several oratorios. All had the substance of the classics combined with romantic imagination and emotion. To understand Robert Schumann, it is important to sample music from each period.

PIANO MUSIC

> Stephen Hough. *Davidsbündlertänze; Album für die Jungend, 21, 26, 30; Fantasie in C.*Virgin Classics (DDD)

This is a good selection of Schumann favorites that show him at his most playful—and most passionate. Hough is an intelligent young artist and a thoughtful interpreter of the work.

> Artur Rubenstein. *Carnaval; Fantasiestücke, Op. 12; Waldscenen; Romance No. 2 for Piano.* RCA (ADD)

Mr. Rubenstein is a grand old master of Schumann performance, and this recording, made in the mid-1960s, displays Rubenstein at his best.

> Murray Perahia. *Piano Sonata No.2 in G minor; (Schubert's Piano sonata No. 20).* CBS (DDD)

A subtle and sensitive recording that makes Schumann's intentions clear, this compact disk also has the advantage of including a great sonata by Schumann's idol, Franz Schubert.

CHAMBER MUSIC

> Beaux Arts Trio, *Quartet in E-flat for Piano and Strings; Quintet in E-flat for Piano and Strings.* Philips (ADD)

This single compact disk contains the two most gorgeous pieces Schumann ever created. His chamber music is rich, warm and confident, and listening to it is guaranteed to generate a warm glow in your ears and your heart.

SYMPHONIC MUSIC

> Murray Perahia. *Piano concerto in A minor;*
> *(Grieg Piano Concerto).* CBS (DDD)

This is usually called the "beloved" romantic concerto, because it has been performed and recorded so often. Some of the finest versions, such as the one recorded by Dinu Lipatti, are not yet available on compact disk, but Perahia has done his work well here.

> Berlin Philharmonic Orchestra. *Symphonies No.*
> *1 (Spring) No. 2, No. 3 (Rhenish), and No. 4.*
> Deutsche Grammophon (ADD)

Every orchestra and conductor interprets these works differently, and if you're serious about Schumann, you'll eventually want to compare different versions. But you may as well start with the best, so begin with the Berlin Philharmonic.

VOCAL MUSIC

> Dietrich Fischer-Dieskau, Baritone. *Dichterliebe;*
> *Liederkreis,* Op. 39. Deutsche Grammophon
> (DDD)

Don't be afraid of *lieder,* these German love songs aren't as difficult to approach as many people think. Read the translated lyrics in the album notes and enjoy the poetry, then sit back and feel the emotional intensity Schumann and Fischer-Dieskau manage to generate.

CLARA SCHUMANN

Frau Schumann spent more time playing concerts and raising her children than she did composing—there are only so many hours in the day. But when she did find time and energy to compose, the results were splendid. Unavailable on recording before 1988, several new releases of her work are now in distribution and more are in preparation. Ask the people at your local classical music store about her newly distributed works.

Clara Wieck Trio. *Piano Trio in G-minor,* (Fanny Mendelssohn-Hensel, *Piano Trio in D.*) Bayer (DDD)

This trio shows Clara Schumann at the height of her creative abilities, and it is generally regarded as her most substantial work.

De Beenhouwer, Jozef. *Complete Works For Piano, Vol 1.* Clara Schumann. Partridge (DDD)

A collection of Frau Schumann's compositions that reaches back to her earliest works as a child prodigy and includes her final composition, the March in E-flat Major. If they seem somehow familiar, it is because her melodies often appear again in the work of Robert Schumann. The two shared musical ideas, with one theme being expanded and developed in many different works.

JOHANNES BRAHMS

Going to the symphony in America means hearing Brahms. You may not walk away from the concert hall humming his tunes, but he is the acknowledged master of the modern symphonic form. Much of his music is *big*, but there is much more to Brahms than his grand and powerful symphonies. When you are shopping for your music library, explore his chamber music and his *lieder* (songs). In these works, Brahms reveals a more lyric, romantic side, which you may find a welcome alternative to the big works.

PIANO MUSIC

Stephen Bishop-Kovacevich. *Seven Fantasias, Three Intermezzi, Four Pieces for Piano.* Philips (DDD)

Brahms' most lyrical, melodic pieces for the piano. Bishop-Kovacevich has recorded three collections of these shorter piano works and all three are excellent.

Emil Gilels; Berlin Philharmonic. *Concerto No. 2 in B-Flat for Piano and Orchestra.* Deutsche Gramaphon (ADD)

Brahms' first piano concerto was ferocious and huge—Hans von Bülow called it "the concerto for piano versus orchestra." The second concerto is bold and big, but not quite as unapproachable. Gilels mastered them both, and his performances are as formidable as the compositions.

CHAMBER MUSIC

Murray Perahia/Amadeus Quartet. *Piano Quartet No. 1 in G minor.* CBS (DDD)

When Vienna heard young Brahms perform his first Piano Quartet, they immediately dubbed him "the young Beethoven." It was a difficult mantle to wear, but he did his best, creating two more Quartets for piano and strings that are considered masterpieces. A young group called *Domus* has also recorded excellent versions of all three on the Virgin Classics label.

SYMPHONIC MUSIC

Fritz Kreisler, Berlin State Opera Orchestra, *Concerto in D for Violin and Orchestra.* Angel (AAD)

Kreisler made this recording in 1929, so don't expect laboratory-quality sound on this compact disk. But a little noise can't cover up the amazing character of this interpretation.

Isaac Stern, Philadelphia Orchestra, *Concerto in D for Violin and Orchestra.* CBS (ADD)

A more modern version of the Violin Concerto reminds us just how easy Isaac Stern can make this difficult piece sound. It is a rich, powerful performance.

˙Heifetz, Piatigorsky, Wallenstein, The RCA Symphony. *Double Concerto in A for Violin, Cello and Orchestra.* RCA (ADD)

Brahms never wrote an opera, but Hans von Bülow said the *Double Concerto* was an opera for two voices, without words. It is certainly lyrical, yet combines those sweet melodies with vintage Brahms power.

VOCAL MUSIC

Margaret Price, Samuel Ramey; Andre Previn and the Royal Philharmonic Orchestra; Ambrosian Singers. *Ein Deutsches Requiem (A German Requiem).* Teldec (DDD)

A magnificent, almost overwhelmingly emotional work that demands absolute attention from the listener. This is not background music.

FRANZ LISZT

History and music critics have not been very kind to the music of Franz Liszt. He was a prodigious composer but few of his major works are seen as having real, lasting musical worth. Virtuoso pianists, however, still love to perform Liszt when they really want to show off, and his

19 *Hungarian Rhapsodies* remain popular favorites. His most important achievement was the invention of a completely new orchestral form, the *symphonic tone poem*. It was a new, romantic kind of composition that threw out all the older, classical conventions of the symphony and let the composer use the orchestra with greater freedom. Of the 13 he wrote, the most commonly heard today is *Les Préludes*.

> Sviatoslav Richter, London Symphony Orchestra. *Piano Concertos Nos. 1 in E-flat and 2 in A.* Philips (AAD)

If you need a powerful dose of Liszt, here is the barnstorming virtuoso at his most ambitious. This version of the piano concertos stays away from most of the bombast and makes the music simply grand and glorious.

> Beecham Choral Society, Royal Philharmonic Orchestra. *A Faust Symphony.* Angel (ADD)

Orchestra, chorus and tenor soloists all team up to present Liszt at his most masterful. Liszt followed in Beethoven's footsteps by adding voice and story to the symphony, and this vintage recording shows how powerful the effect could be. If you want a modern, fully digital recording, EMI has an excellent version by the Westminster College Male Chorus and the Philadelphia Orchestra.

RICHARD WAGNER

Wagner's theoretical *Music of the Future* imagined an opera that was a complete synthesis of music, drama and art. He would be the first to agree that the only way to really absorb this total experience is at a live performance. But your opportunities to sit through *Götterdämmerung* may be limited, so you probably will want to supplement your experience with some recorded Wagner. Consider choosing one of the collections of excerpts, some with vocal selections, some limited to orchestral arrangements. Let your conscience be your guide.

> Cleveland Orchestra. *Overtures and Preludes from The Flying Dutchman, The Meistersinger of Nürnberg, Tannhäuser, Tristan and Isolde.* CBS (ADD)

> New York Philharmonic. *Vocal and Orchestral Excerpts from Der Ring des Nibelungen: Entry of the Gods; Ride of the Valkyries; Magic Fire Music; Immolation Scene and others.* CBS (DDD)

> Behrens, Minton, Hofmann, Weikl, Sotin, Bernstein, Bavarian Radio Symphony and Chorus. *Tristan und Isolde (The Complete Opera in Three Acts)* Philips (DDD)

If you're going to get one complete Wagnerian opera, try this one. The opera is Wagner's most magnificent work, Leonard Bernstein conducts with amazing style. The vocal work of Hildegard Behrens and Peter Hofmann are of the highest quality.

A MUSICAL VOCABULARY

MAJOR MUSICAL FORMS

Classical composers worked within the strict framework of standard musical forms. Carefully defined rules of composition were taught to each young musician, who then went on to write proper sonatas, minuets and suites. Romantic musicians didn't abandon those forms, they just loosened the rules a little, adding different types of compositions with fewer restrictions and more room for musical expression.

CLASSICAL FORMS

SONATA

An extended instrumental work for solo piano or solo instrument and piano. It is usually composed of three or four *movements*, self-contained but interrelated. The first movement of a sonata is written in the *sonata form*, an architectural design that is also used in the concerto, the symphony and the string quartet. It begins with the statement of the principal theme, moves through a period of development and enlargement and then restates the same theme to close the movement. A *sonatina* is just like a sonata, only shorter.

CONCERTO

A grand work for solo performer and orchestra, designed to show off the talents of the soloist. It is also possible to have a *double concerto* for two performers and orchestra, or even a *string quartet concerto* for four performers. The first movement is usually in the sonata form, the second is often a theme and variation or a song form and the third movement is lively, frequently in the *rondo* dance form.

STRING QUARTET

An extended work for two violins, viola and cello. The form is generally the same as a symphony, only with lower overhead. Adding another viola makes it a string quintet. Adding a piano makes it a piano quintet.

SYMPHONY

A major work for a large orchestra, usually composed of the same four types of movements found in the sonata or the concerto. Mozart and Haydn always made the third movement a *minuet,* but Beethoven replaced the old dance form with a more sophisticated *scherzo.* The last movement can be a *rondo,* a theme and variation or it can move back to the old standard sonata form.

SUITE

One of the oldest classical forms, the suite's popularity began during the baroque period, but its roots extend back into ancient times. A suite is a collection of old dance forms, usually beginning with an *allemande* and ending with a *gigue.*

DANCES USED IN CLASSICAL SUITES

Allemande	German peasant dance.
Bourée	Ancient French or Spanish court dance.

Chaconne	A slow and sedate old Spanish dance.
Gavotte	An old French dance.
Gigue	An old English dance that later became the jig.
Minuet	A stately French court dance.
Passepied	A lively French dance like a fast minuet.
Polonaise	A Polish national dance.
Sarabande	A dignified old Spanish dance.

OTHER DANCE FORMS USED IN COMPOSITION

Bolero	A Spanish dance with seductive, repeated rhythms.
Fandango	An energetic Spanish dance that sounds like it should be accompanied by castanets.
Habanera	A slow, sensuous dance from Spain's colony of Havana, Cuba.
Mazurka	A Polish national dance popularized by Chopin.
Rondo	A round dance that repeats the main theme again and again. This form is often used as the last movement of sonatas and concertos.
Tarantella	An Italian sailor's dance filled with speed, excitement and a sense of danger.
Waltz	Invented by Austrian peasants, this dance was perfected in Vienna and ultimately took Europe by storm.

FUGUE

The fugue is the most complex form of _counterpoint_ produced during the baroque period. Modern singers demonstrate the simplest form of counterpoint when they sing rounds like _Row, row row your boat._ Bach and his contemporaries in the 17th century developed counterpoint to a high art, with fugues of amazing mathematical complexity that combined as many as five different voices weaving around each other.

MASS

The most solemn ritual of the Catholic church is often accompanied by music. The earliest masses were for choir without instruments. As the form developed, the Mass became a major production, including solo voice, choir and orchestra. The six major parts of the mass are: _Kyrie, Gloria, Credo, Sanctus, Benedictus_ and _Agnus Dei,_ following the order of the service. After the Protestant reformation, music continued in the form of _hymns, chorales_ and _oratorios._

ORATORIO

A major work for soloists, choir and orchestra based on a biblical text. The oratorio is rather like a religious opera without costumes or scenery.

OPERA

A musical drama in which the plot is moved forward only through music. The opera integrates song and story completely, as opposed to an _operetta,_ where the story moves along on its own and is occasionally punctuated with songs.

MODERN INNOVATIONS

The romantics added some new forms to the composer's repertoire.

CONCERT OVERTURE

Originally designed to be the prelude of a play or opera, the overture eventually went on to assume a life of its own.

FANTASIA

An old form that goes back to the baroque music of Bach, a fantasia is a whim or fancy that gives the composer maximum freedom of expression. Anything can go into a fantasia.

IMPROMPTU

A short piece that is spontaneous and unstructured, rather like a song sung in the shower.

NOCTURNE

A poetic, expressionistic piece filled with dreams and passionate melodies.

RHAPSODY

A new form invented by the early romantics and popularized by Liszt, the rhapsody is a gay, emotional piece filled with poetry and passion. Often, rhapsodies are based on folk tunes or popular melodies.

SYMPHONIC POEM

A one-movement symphonic work with a very elastic form that gives the composer maximum freedom. Franz

Liszt invented the term and used the form to tell stories or paint musical pictures.

PERFORMANCE INSTRUCTIONS

Each movement of a musical composition is marked with instructions from the composer about how it should be played. The vocabulary is largely Italian but the language is universal, and classical musicians all over the world understand when Mozart marks a Sonata *Allegro Moderato* or Schumann indicates that his *Fantasia* should be played *Sempre fantasticamente ed appassionatamente*.

VOCABULARY

Accelerando	Speed up
Adagio	Very slowly
Agitato	Agitated and hurried
Allegretto	Slower than allegro, but quickly
Allegro	Lively and quick
Andante	Medium slow
Appassionata	Passionately
Brio	With spirit
Crescendo	Getting gradually louder
Decrescendo	Getting gradually softer
Dolce	Sweetly
Doloroso	Sadly
Fantasticament	Fantasticly
Feroce	Fiercely
Forte	Loud
Fortissimo	Very loud
Fortississimo	Very, very loud
Grave	Gravely
Langsam	Nobly
Largo	Slowly
Legato	Smooth and connected

Lento	Slowly, but not as slowly as Largo
Lesto	Lively
Maestoso	Majestic
Maliconia	Melancholy
Moderato	Moderate time
Molto	Very
Mosso	Rapid
Piano	Soft
Pianissimo	Very soft
Pianississimo	Very, very soft
Placido	Placidly
Poco	Little
Presto	Very fast
Rallentando	Becoming slower
Sempre	Always
Tempo	Time
Troppo	Too much
Veloce	Swift
Vivace	Lively
Vivo	Animated

A READER'S BIBLIOGRAPHY

GENERAL INFORMATION

Dahlhaus, Carl. *Ninteenth-Century Music.* Translated by J. Bradford Robinson. Berekely, Los Angeles: University of California Press, 1989.

The Dahlhaus writing style reminds one of Wagner's prose—complex, convoluted and almost incomprehensible. The translation doesn't help much either. It seems likely that the author also shares Wagner's musical views, if we can judge by his low opinion of Brahms and Schumann. This book is an excellent choice if you need to catch up on your sleep.

Plantinga, Leon. *Romantic Music, A History of Musical Style in Nineteenth-Century Europe.* New York & London: W. W. Norton & Company, 1984.

A comprehensive and easily understood study of romantic music from its roots to its results. Plantinga is careful to look at the economic and social factors that influence musical changes, as well as explaining the structure and style of great works.

Rosenstiel, Léonie, general ed. *Schirmer History of Music,* Griffel, L. Michael, ed. *The Romantic and Post-Romantic Eras.* New York: Schirmer Books, 1982.

An excellent, readable text if you would like to learn more about music and the events that shaped its history. It begins with Aristotle and ends with electronic synthesizers. The chapters focusing on romanticism are illuminating.

> Sadie, Stanley, ed. *The Norton/Grove Encyclopedia of Music*, New York & London: W.W.Norton & Company, 1988.

The original *New Grove Dictionary of Music and Musicians* (1980) is a 20-volume masterpiece. This version is only 850 pages long, but still contains more than most amateurs will ever want to know about music. It includes brief biographies of everyone from Benny Goodman to Yehudi Menuhin, definitions of musical terms and concepts, the plots of operas and a wealth of other information.

THE PEOPLE

CLARA SCHUMANN

> Reich, Nancy B. *Clara Schumann: The Artist and the Woman*. Ithaca and London: Cornell University Press, 1985.

An exhaustive and very scholarly study that's still a good read. Reich doesn't place Clara on an ivory pedestal, as the Victorian biographers did. Neither is she limited to viewing Clara only through her husband's career. We get an honest look at a brilliant, sometimes difficult woman with incredible energy and single-minded determination.

Burk, John N. *Clara Schumann: A Romantic Biography.* New York: Random House, 1941.

This is the old-style, rose-colored glasses version of Robert and Clara Schumann, complete with engraved love birds. It, or one like it, is probably the only biography you'll find at the public library.

ROBERT SCHUMANN

Niecks, Frederick. Edited By Christina Niecks, J.M. Dent & Sons Ltd. *Robert Schumann: A Supplementary and Corrective Biography.* New York: E.P. Dutton & Co. 1925.

This book was a first attempt to write an accurate, rather than worshipful, biography. The style is old-fashioned, but Niecks does try to get at the truth.

Schauffler, Robert Haven. *Florestan: The Life and Work of Robert Schumann.* New York: Henry Holt and Company, 1945.

More rose-colored glasses, but the sections on Schumann's music are excellent and surprisingly objective.

Schumann, Robert. Edited by Konrad Wolff and translated byPaul Rosenfeld. *On Music and Musicians.* New York, Toronto and London: McGraw-Hill Book Company, 1964.

Schumann, Robert. Translated and edited by Henry Pleasants. *Schumann on Music: A Selection from the Writings.* New York: Dover Publications, Inc., 1965.

Both of these books give us a chance to see what kind of a writer Robert Schumann really was. George Bernard Shaw once accused Schumann of being a *musical enthusiast* rather than a *music critic*, and his enthusiasm is clear in these articles. But he can hit hard when the occasion merits. The biggest surprise is how genuinely funny he can be, even in translation.

Walker, Alan, ed. *Robert Schumann: The Man and his Music*. London: Barrie and Jenkins, 1972.

This collection of articles and essays includes the most recent medical theories on the cause of Schumann's final illness.

Walker, Alan. *Schumann*. London: Faber and Faber, 1976.

A short, powerful and accurate retelling of Schumann's life. Walker is an objective, insightful biographer.

JOHANNES BRAHMS

Geiringer, Karl in collaboration with Irene Geiringer. *Brahms: His Life and Work.* Da Capo Press, 1982.

If you want the interesting parts of Brahms life in an easy-to-read package, Geiringer is the best of the biographies still available in print.

MacDonald, Malcolm. *Brahms*. New York: Schirmer Books, a Division of Macmillan Inc., 1990.

The newest and most definitive of Brahms' biographies, MacDonald is factual but boring.

Schauffler, Robert Haven. *The Unknown Brahms: His Life, Character and Works. Based on New Material.* New York: Dodd, Mead and Company, 1934.

This is where one can find the best information about Brahms' early sexual misadventures and his affection for Vienna's ladies of the night. Good, well-substantiated gossip.

FRANZ LISZT

Newman, Ernest. *The Man Liszt: A Study of the Tragi-Comedy of A Soul Divided Against Itself.* New York: Taplinger Publishing Company, 1935.

No one knows quite why Ernest Newman hated Liszt, but he must have had a deep-seated grudge. This is not so much a biography as an assault and battery. Newman drug up every unsubstantiated rumor ever circulated about Liszt and carefully categorized his every fault and failure. A lot of this stuff is patently false, but it's still fascinating.

Perényi, Eleanor. *Liszt: The Artist As Romantic Hero.* Boston-Toronto: Little, Brown and Company, 1974.

Good, honest gossip makes a great biography, and Perény has written a wonderful, admittedly subjective, account of Liszt's life. Objective or not, her facts are accurate, but mysteriously, she ends her story 20 years before his death.

Sitwell, Sacheverell. *Liszt.* New York: Dover Publications, Inc., 1967.

Dover has reprinted this biography which Sitwell originally wrote in 1935, the same year as Newman's character assassination. Some critics have called this the defense case and Newman the prosecution.

Watson, Derek. *Liszt.* New York: Schirmer Books, 1989.

This is a no-nonsense biography that doesn't let itself get bogged down in personalities.

COSIMA LISZT VON BÜLOW WAGNER

Gregor-Dellin, Martin and Dietrich Mack, eds. *Cosima Wagner's Diaries 1869-1877. Volume One* and Cosima *Wagner's Diaries 1878-1883. Volume Two.* New York and London: Harcourt Brace Jovanovich, 1976.

You may find it difficult to read much of this, because her constant self-criticism and dependent obsession with Wagner are almost pathetic. But if you stumble across a copy in the library or a used book store, read a few chapters. This is a fascinating chronicle of a neurotic relationship.

Sokoloff, Alice Hunt. *Cosima Wagner: Extraordinary daughter of Franz Liszt.* New York: Dodd, Mead & Company, 1969.

The best available biography of Cosima. It leaves out a few scenes that show Wagner behaving badly, but provides a reasonably accurate picture of their life together.

A READER'S BIBLIOGRAPHY

RICHARD WAGNER

Barth, Herbert, Dietrich Mack and Egon Voss, eds. *Wagner: A Documentary Study*. New York: Oxford University Press, 1975.

Sometimes it's best to just let Wagner speak in his own voice, especially in letters and conversations where he lets down his guard and reveals his real personality. This book lets Wagner speak for himself.

Chancellor, John. *Wagner*. Boston Toronto: Little, Brown and Company, 1978.

A clear, readable biography that's not too worshipful—a common problem in Wagner literature.

Gutman, Robert W. *Richard Wagner: The Man, His Mind, and His Music*. San Diego New York London: Harcourt Brace Javanovich, 1990.

The newest, and most objective, of the Wagner biographies. This one is rigorously detached and nonjudgemental, as well as exhaustive in its look at the composer.

Howard, John Tasker. *The World's Great Operas*. New York: The Modern Library, 1959.

A tiny little book with one-page summaries of all the great opera libretti, including Wagner's. The stories are interesting, but reading them will remind you why the music is always more important than the plot.

Magee, Bryan. *Aspects of Wagner*. Oxford, New York: Oxford University Press, 1988.

These short essays are not classical biography, but they are wonderfully insightful, Magee may help you understand what made Wagner tick in a way no other biographer could.

Millington, Barry. *Wagner.* New York: Vintage Books, 1987.

His facts are good and the text moves along smartly, but Millington is far too willing to explain away Wagner's behavior. You may find it hard to be that forgiving.

Wagner, Richard. Translated by Andrew Gray, edited by Mary Whittal. *Mein Leben (My Life).* Cambridge: Cambridge University Press, 1983.

Most of Wagner's writing is almost impossible to follow, but this autobiography is actually readable. Because King Ludwig commissioned the work and asked Cosima to help with the task, it's probable that she wrote a lot of it. As a result, Wagner's life has been sanitized a great deal, but this is still remarkably honest—for Wagner.

LISTENING RECOMMENDATIONS

Svejda, Jim. *The Record Shelf Guide to the Classical Repertoire.* Rocklin, CA: Prima Publishing.

Svejda is knowledgeable, funny and opinionated. He offers sage advice on selecting the works of composers, performers and conductors.

Greenfield, Edward, Robert Layton and Ivan March. *The Penguin Guide To Compact Discs.* Penguin Books

An exhaustive list of recordings that may, or may not, bear listening to. The editors provide lots of guidance to help you decide.